ABORT ABORTION

MARK DRISCOLL

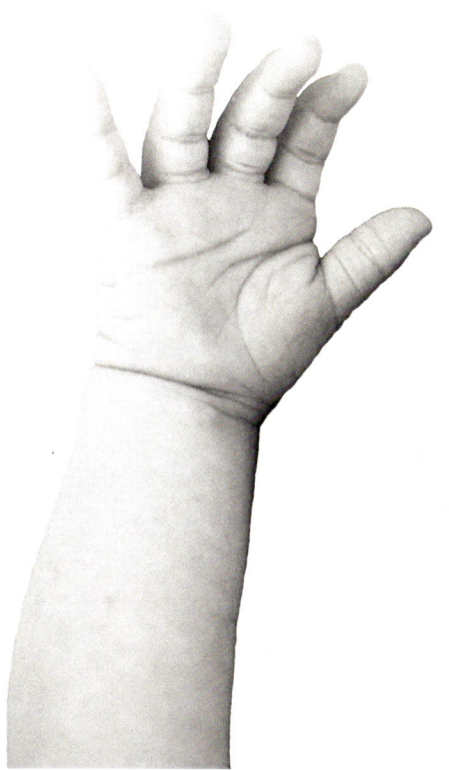

Abort Abortion
© 2022 by Mark Driscoll

ISBN: 979-8-9863100-2-2 (Paperback)
ISBN: 979-8-9863100-3-9 (E-book)

Unless otherwise indicated, scripture quotations are from The Holy Bible, English Standard Version, copyright 2001 by Crossway Bibles, a publishing ministry of Good News Publishers. Used by permission. All rights reserved.

All emphases in Scripture quotations have been added by the author.

No part of this publication may be reproduced, stored in a retrieval system, or transmitted in any form by any means, electronic, mechanical, photocopy, recording, or otherwise, without the prior permission of the publisher, except as provided for by USA copyright law.

CONTENTS

INTRODUCTION: GRACE FROM MY WIFE GRACE V

PREFACE: I WAS PRO-ABORTION IX

CHAPTER ONE: ROE RAGE 1

CHAPTER TWO: SEX IS A RELIGION, LGBTQIA ARE DENOMINATIONS, AND ABORTION IS A DEMONIC COUNTERFEIT SACRIFICE 11

CHAPTER THREE: FOLLOW THE SCIENCE...LIFE BEGINS AT CONCEPTION 21

CHAPTER FOUR: HUMAN LIFE IS UNIQUELY SACRED 35

CHAPTER FIVE: 27 SCRIPTURES ABOUT THE UNBORN 47

CHAPTER SIX: GOD BECAME A ZYGOTE 59

CHAPTER SEVEN: CHRISTIANS HAVE ALWAYS BEEN PRO-LIFE 69

CHAPTER EIGHT: HOW THE WOMB BECAME A TOMB 77

POSTSCRIPT: WHAT HAPPENS TO ME, AND MY BABY, IF I HAD AN ABORTION? 97

INTRODUCTION: GRACE FROM MY WIFE GRACE

Romans 8:1 (NLT) — So now there is no condemnation for those who belong to Christ Jesus.

Have you ever done something or had something done to you that you wish wasn't a part of your life story? You are not alone. We all have parts of our life story that the Enemy wants to use to shame us, condemn us, and isolate us with. If you have had an abortion, whether you chose it or someone chose it for you, whether you knew what you were doing or you are just realizing the tragic facts…Jesus has healing, not condemnation, for you. There is not a sin that His death on the cross didn't cover. It's not the unpardonable sin. As a pastor's kid and a pastor's wife, I have listened to and cried with many women during their healing process who have previously had abortions. I've been the first person some women have told. There have been tens of millions of abortions which means tens of millions of women have emotional (and often physical) pain, whether they acknowledge it or not. I have heard the guilt of "How could I have done that?", "I can never forgive myself", "How could God forgive me?", "Why didn't anyone tell me what it really was?", "I thought there was no other option", and "My boyfriend said I had to." These are all heartbreaking feelings that women hold on to for years, as the shame tells them they are alone and unforgivable.

    Grieving the loss and working through the pain of taking your baby's life can be a daunting thought. Isn't keeping it a secret easier? Isn't numbing the feelings and moving on the best solution? It won't affect the rest of my life, right? I wish the answer could be a simple yes and you could move on. But just like any sin or brokenness in our life, if we don't work through it with the Lord (and healthy Christian community), it will be a dark place in our soul that keeps popping up and brings anxiety, doubt, anger, and insecurity, rather than freedom, forgiveness, joy, and confidence in God's love for us. God doesn't love us for what we do or not do, He loves us because He created us in His image and wants an abundant life for us. We are not saved by our good works, and if we love Jesus, we aren't condemned for our bad works either. Forgiveness is a powerful process that offers freedom from past, present, and future sins…all done by Jesus' death on the cross and resurrection which brings us new life! The world has lied to us, but God gives us truth that sets us free. I encourage you to ask Jesus to walk this healing path with you. Grab a journal, your Bible, and some Kleenex. Pray and start writing your story and whatever comes to mind. Be honest about the pain, the lies, and the feelings that emerge. Ask God to forgive you, heal you, and take the condemnation of the Enemy from you, and this will start the process of grieving and walking in freedom! In case you're wondering, Jesus has already forgiven you, but we have to take the steps to WALK IN FORGIVENESS. You are loved by the God who created you! The promise of Hebrews 4:16 (NLT) is for you, "So let us come boldly to the throne of our gracious God. There we will receive mercy, and we will find grace to help us when we need it most."

    Lastly, a godly Christian counselor filled with the Spirit who will pray for you and walk with you could be a big part of your healing journey. I would also recommend the following resource to help with your healing: "Surrendering the Secret: Healing the Heartbreak of Abortion", by Patricia Layton.

You are loved by the God who created you, and in Him you are a new creation!

Grace Driscoll

PREFACE: I WAS PRO-ABORTION

Romans 12:2 (NLT) – Don't copy the behavior and customs of this world, but let God transform you into a new person by changing the way you think. Then you will learn to know God's will for you, which is good and pleasing and perfect.

Growing up as the oldest of five children in a Catholic family, you would have thought that I would have been pro-life like my parents and their church. Instead, I was the complete opposite.

As a child, I was curious, so I would often ride my bike a lengthy distance to our local library to check out magazines and books to learn about the world. We lived next to an airport, and as the planes flew overhead, I always wondered where they were going and what life was like in the places they landed.

As a kid at the library, I somehow stumbled across magazines and books that were pro-abortion and they caught my attention. I started reading out of curiosity but then eventually came to believe the persuasive arguments that an unborn child was not yet a full human life, that our world was headed toward overpopulation which could lead to harming or even ending the human race, that humans evolved from lower life forms, that some people were genetically less fit and a threat to the continued evolution of the human species, and that human sexuality without any constraints or restraints was an essential freedom for humanity. To me, it made sense to not encourage any constraints or restraints on human sexuality, that we should limit human population with birth control and that unwanted pregnancies, especially those with less fit offspring, should be terminated through abortion. To me, this case against life was compelling and even morally virtuous for a good humanity.

In high school where I was the Student Body President and did a lot of public speaking, in one of my larger classes, students were paired off to debate an issue and got to pick which issue they preferred. A sweet Christian girl asked to debate me on abortion. She chose the pro-life side of the debate, and halfway through our debate she burst into tears and ran out of the classroom devastated because I had burned every one of her arguments to the ground.

In this same season, I met another sweet Christian girl whose dad was a pastor. I quickly grew very fond of her, and we started dating. During one of our times together, the issue of abortion came up and she had very clear and very devout pro-life views. I poked holes in her reasoning but did not have a heated debate because I wanted to continue dating her. Occasionally, the issue would arise, and we would have a brief, kind discussion that ended in neither of us budging on our views, and then we'd move on.

In college, I was studying under an avowedly Marxist professor as a freshman. I spent time out of class with him learning more about such things as abortion, economic transference of wealth by the government to create equity, and other issues that have become the woke progressive political agenda today. He further instructed me on the eugenics ideology of Thomas Malthus that was held by Margaret Sanger, the founder of Planned Parenthood, and it seemed logical to me. I wrongly believed less fit people should be sterilized, not permitted to conceive, and encouraged to abort if they became pregnant. In our large class, he asked if some students would be willing to prepare for a public debate on these kinds of issues, and some students volunteered to do so, while the shy kids did not raise their hand. I was eager for a verbal joust, and so he assigned me the issue of abortion. On the day of the debate, things in college went pretty much the same way as they had in high school. The nice Christian student got melted to the ground and could not finish our debate as they were in tears.

Around this same time, I started reading the Bible the pastor's daughter gave me out of curiosity. It seemed every class I took at the state university was anti-Christian. Because I really did care about the pastor's daughter who was now my girlfriend, and she had bought me a very nice leather-bound Bible with my name on it, I felt like the least I could do was read it a bit to see what it said.

I was quickly confronted with the worldview of the Bible. It seemed clear to me that, according to the Bible, pretty much everything I thought about God, myself, and life on our planet was wrong. I decided that either the Bible was wrong, or I was wrong, but that there was no way to reconcile what I had been taught and what the Bible taught.

In this season, God brought some Christian students into my life who brought me to a Bible study with their pastor who had a PhD and was a very humble and brilliant man of God. I also took a philosophy class with a professor who told us he was a Bible-believing Christian. These two men kindly started spending time with me to teach me the Bible and why it was superior to competing ideologies.

I became a Christian reading the Bible that the pastor's daughter gave me. She knew that when we were arguing, she was right but that I would win the argument. Sadly, this is often the case as the lie wins the argument and the truth loses. She knew that if she could get me to argue with the Bible instead of other people, I would lose my debate with God and His Word. She was right.

The pastor's daughter moved to attend college with me, and she volunteered her time at the local pro-life crisis pregnancy clinic helping other young women making difficult decisions. I married that pastor's daughter in 1992 and began preaching through books of the Bible in 1996. Today, we have five wonderful children that we adore and enjoy. Today, I cannot imagine what I was thinking when Grace gave me that Bible. To think that God might've had to save our own children from me is a terrifying thing to consider. With two married children, and the prospect of what could be a lot of grandkids one day, the thought of killing my blessings brings me to tears.

With the overturning of the landmark abortion case Roe v Wade now in the headlines, and a massive national and even global debate about abortion around Roe rage, I am writing this book to share some thoughts as a Bible-believing Christian, husband, and father in hopes of helping other people not only respect life but meet God, who is the author of life. This book is free thanks to the wonderful ministry partners at realfaith.com. There is no publisher so it cannot be cancelled, and there are no endorsers so they cannot be attacked. I'm praying for all who read it, as I started on the right side of history but wrong side of eternity and want to help others cross that line in repentance.

Lastly, I want to thank God the Holy Spirit for prompting me to write this book. I was in the mountains of Arizona for a day off and hike when I felt compelled to write this book, so I sat down for 14 consecutive hours praying and writing. This book was written in that one sitting with new revelation from the Scriptures I had not seen before, which was a wonderful time of worship for my soul.

A voice in the desert,

ROE RAGE

Matthew 19:14 (ESV) – Jesus said, "Let the little children come to me and do not hinder them, for to such belongs the kingdom of heaven."

When I was born in 1970, abortion was not yet nationally legalized. Then, in January 1973, the U.S. Supreme Court decided on an infamous case now known as Roe v Wade.

Wade was in reference to the district attorney Henry Wade of Dallas County, Texas. The pseudonym "Roe" covered the identity of Norma McCorvey, a woman from Louisiana who filed a lawsuit in Texas to get an abortion, which was illegal in that state at that time. Curiously, she later became a Christian and has spent much of her adult life speaking out against abortion, painfully recalling her regret as she thankfully found grace and healing in Jesus Christ.

The Court justices ruled that states could not ban abortions prior to the viability of the child, which the court at the time determined to be 24-28 weeks into pregnancy. Today, considering medical advancements, that timeframe is shorter as children born before this window have lived. The linchpin for the Court was the "right to privacy" which the court interpreted from the Due Process Clause of the 14th Amendment and applied to women seeking abortions by a 7-2 vote of all male justices.

Roe v Wade legalized abortion throughout the entire United

States for the first time in the nation's history and was a seismic legal shift. Although a few states already had legalized abortions in some cases (e.g. New York, Hawaii, Colorado), this changed the national landscape regarding abortion. Abortion has since peaked in the U.S. at around 1.4 million a year.

Even those on the political left who favor abortion have acknowledged the legal weakness of the decision. Former liberal Justice Ruth Bader Ginsburg said that with Roe the Court, "ventured too far in the change it ordered and presented an incomplete justification for its action".[1] She went on to call it "heavy-handed judicial intervention"[2]

Other legal experts have also criticized Roe as legally weak, even if they morally agree with it. Laurence Tribe said in the Harvard Law Review, "One of the most curious things about Roe is that, behind its own verbal smokescreen, the substantive judgment on which it rests is nowhere to be found."[3] Edward Lazarus, who is the former clerk to Harry Blackmun (he authored the Roe v Wade opinion) said, "As a matter of constitutional interpretation and judicial method, Roe borders on the indefensible. I say this as someone utterly committed to the right to choose..."[4] Kermit Roosevelt from the University of Pennsylvania Law School said, "[I]t is time to admit in public that, as an example of the practice of constitutional opinion writing, Roe is a serious disappointment. You will be hard-pressed to find a constitutional law professor, even among those who support the idea of constitutional protection for the right to choose, who will embrace the opinion itself rather than the result. This is not surprising. As constitutional argument, Roe is barely coherent. The court pulled its fundamental right to choose more or less from the constitutional ether..."[5]

Liberal legal minds have been concerned about the weakness of the Roe v Wade case for years. Even those who agree with abortion see the legal underpinnings as akin to what Jesus called building a house on sand.

Almost 20 years later, the Roe v Wade verdict was challenged in the Casey v Planned Parenthood case. The Court's decision was that states could make restrictions on abortions but could not force an "undue burden" on a woman seeking an abortion for a not-yet-viable unborn child.

In a breach of confidentiality that is essential for due legal process, a draft memo that indicated Roe v Wade might be headed toward being overturned was released to the public May 3, 2022. This immediately caused an eruption on both sides of the debate, with people taking to the internet and streets to argue their case for and against abortion.

Many people, however, seem confused about what happens if/when Roe v Wade is overturned. This does not automatically mean that abortion is illegal across America. Instead, the issue will be sent back to the states, with each state needing to determine its own laws regarding abortion. In some states, there are trigger laws that would automatically outlaw abortions in the second and third trimesters if/when Roe v Wade is overturned. Some states would take a more moderated approach and disallow abortions after a certain number of weeks, such as 15. More liberal states would allow abortion up until birth. In short, there will be a heated ongoing debate and political battle in every state on the issue, with various states reaching a variety of legal conclusions.

The most liberal abortion advocates would also prefer allowing abortion up through birth, which is simply the murder of infanticide, something we should expect to eventually see following the overturning of Roe v Wade. For example, CNN reported in 2019, "Virginia Democratic Gov. Ralph Northam is facing backlash after he voiced his support for a state measure that would significantly loosen restrictions on late-term abortions. '[Third trimester abortions are] done in cases where there may be severe deformities. There may be a fetus that's nonviable. So in this particular example, if a mother is in labor, I can tell you exactly what would happen,'" Northam, a pediatric neurosurgeon, told Washington radio station WTOP. "The infant would be delivered. The infant would be kept comfortable. The infant would be resuscitated if that's what the mother and the family desired. And then a discussion would ensue between the physicians and the mother."[6]

To be clear, he is advocating that a child who is born alive but struggling to live, would only be resuscitated if the "mother and family desired". Can you imagine anyone in a hospital only being given life-saving medical attention if the family asked for it? Even criminals wounded while committing crimes are given the dignity of life-saving health measures, but apparently not newborn children. If a born child lives, "then a discussion would ensue between the physicians and the mother" – about whether or not to terminate or permit the born living child to continue to live. When you start with flawed assumptions and follow them to their logical conclusion this is the literal dead end that is inevitable once your mind, conscience, and soul are seared by the same fires that keep hell burning.

MEDICAL MURDER

The Bible makes a distinction between crimes and sins. Crimes are against the government while sins are against God. This explains why you can call the police if someone assaults you or steals from you, but they will not respond if you say that someone was unloving toward you or got drunk in your apartment.

God's laws transcend and expect more of God's people than the laws of government. If someone claims to be a Christian, as President Joe Biden does, then they are to not only obey the laws of government, but also of God. The more authority God gives us, the more responsibility we bear to do what is right in the sight of God.

When it comes to abortion, it is far more important to be on the right side of eternity than the right side of history.

In an article I wrote for Fox News some years ago, I said this regarding abortion: "Of all the Ten Commandments, number six is the only one that our nation has codified into law. 'You shall not murder.'"

Even pro-abortion, feminist, non-Christian Naomi Wolf admitted this in her 1996 article, "Our Bodies, Our Souls."[7] She starts her articulate and honest article saying, "I had an abortion when I was a single mother and my daughter was 2 years old." She goes and admits, "Clinging to a rhetoric about abortion in which there is no life and death, we entangle our beliefs in a series of self-delusions, fibs, and evasions." She "admits that the death of a fetus is a real death" and the high number of abortions are "a failure" although she admits it is an "evil-necessary evil". She goes on to confess, "the pro-life slogan, 'Abortion stops a beating heart,' is incontrovertibly true" and recognizes the "personhood" of an unborn child, and "the humanity of the fetus". When asked, while considering an abortion during her pregnancy, what her answer was when someone asked if she was "with child", she said, "Of course, it's a baby." She goes on to admit that "We on the left tend to twitch with discomfort at that word 'sin'" but sees it as a potential doorway to healing, not unlike the Christian gospel saying, "our recognition of sin, and then atonement for it, brings on God's compassion and our redemption" to explain how to "live with a conscious view that abortion is an evil and still be pro-choice…"

When talking about abortion, it is helpful to understand exactly how this gruesome murderous procedure occurs. These are the methods of abortion to help you understand how we kill our kids. It is quoted directly from a Christian theological journal:[8]

SUCTION ASPIRATION

This procedure is used in 80 percent of the abortions up to the 12th week of pregnancy. The mouth of the cervix is dilated. A hollow tube with a knifelike edged tip is inserted into the womb. A suction force 28 times stronger than a vacuum cleaner literally tears the developing baby to pieces and sucks the remains into a container.

DILATION AND CURETTAGE

Dilation and curettage (commonly called D & C) is a procedure which involves dilating the cervix with a series of instruments to allow the insertion of a curette—a loop-shaped knife—into the womb. The instrument is used to scrape the placenta from the uterus and then cut the baby apart. The pieces are then drawn through the cervix. The tiny body must then be reassembled by an attending nurse to make sure no parts remain in the womb to cause infection.

SALINE INJECTION

Saline injection, also known as "salt-poisoning," is an abortion procedure which involves removing some of the amniotic fluid surrounding the baby and replacing it with a toxic, saline solution. The baby then breathes and swallows the solution. In one or two hours the unborn child dies from salt poisoning, dehydration, and hemorrhaging. The mother goes into labor about 24 hours later and delivers a dead (or dying) baby.

HYSTERONOMY

During the last three months of pregnancy, abortions are performed by hysterotomy, which involves opening the womb surgically and removing the baby as in a Caesarean section. However, the purpose of this procedure is to end the infant's life. Instead of being cared for, the baby is wrapped in a blanket, set aside, and allowed to die.

PROSTAGLANDIN

This newest abortion procedure involves the use of chemicals developed by the Upjohn Pharmaceutical Company. Prostaglandin hormones, injected into the womb or released in a vaginal suppository, cause the uterus to contract, and deliver the child prematurely—too young to survive. A saline solution is sometimes injected first, killing the baby before birth, in order to make the procedure less distressful for the mother and medical staff.[9]

The question is then asked, "Do the unborn feel pain during these abortion procedures?" Yes, they do. Dr. A. W. Liley, world-renowned professor of Fetal Physiology at the National Women's Hospital in Auckland, New Zealand, has shown that the unborn child can feel pain and is sensitive to touch, light, heat, and noise as early as 11 weeks after conception.[10]

We then learn, "Using closed-circuit TV cameras, he has shown that if the unborn child is pricked with a needle, the infant will recoil in pain. But if a beep sounds before the prick, and this is repeated several times, the tiny baby will begin to recoil at the beep in anticipation of the pain he knows will come."[11]

In addition to these medical abortions that have been in effect for decades, "In 2016 the U.S. Food and Drug Administration approved a two-drug combination of Mifeprex (also called RU-486 or mifepristone) and Cytotec (commonly known as misoprostol) to induce abortion without surgery. In 2019 the Centers for Disease Control and Prevention reported that approximately 42 percent of all abortions in the U.S. were medication-based. To start the process, a person takes mifepristone within seven weeks from their last period. One or two days later, they take misoprostol. If mifepristone isn't available, misoprostol can work alone. Mifepristone blocks progesterone's action on the uterus, making it incapable of supporting a pregnancy. Misoprostol, among other things, starts uterine contractions."[12]

WE TREAT OUR PETS BETTER THAN OUR KIDS

Now, compare how we treat our kids to how we treat our pets.[13]

In most U.S. states, you can kill your pet to relieve their pain under specific circumstances if you meet two criteria. Failure to comply with these laws that protect against animal cruelty can result in jail time, probation, or fines.

One, you can kill your pet if it is so injured or sick that it is suffering and near death. However, unlike a baby, "it is illegal to kill your pet for no reason".

Two, you can kill your pet if they are "not fit" for living. Examples would include severe brain damage, or a pet at risk of losing multiple limbs, or otherwise unable to functionally live.

Unlike an abortion, which a minor can receive without parental consent in many states, "Most owners consult with a veterinarian before determining if an animal is near death or unfit for living a long and healthy life."[14]

Let's say your dog is so sick that you need to kill them. Laws generally require that it A) be done in a humane way and B) use a way that is painless, fast, and effective. Tragically, the same cannot be said for an unborn child.

To further show that the life of a pet is worth more than the life of a child, "If your dog could have a decent standard of living for several years, you can't kill them. Killing a healthy and happy animal yourself is always considered illegal."[15]

To protect the sacred life of pets, the American Veterinary Medical Association (AVMA) has "guidelines for the euthanasia of animals". At 121 pages, it is a thoughtful, extensive, and compassionate set of guidelines for everything from dogs to cats, as well as bunnies and rats, among other animals.[16]

The goal is, "As veterinarians and human beings it is our responsibility to ensure that if an animal's life is to be taken, it is done with the highest degree of respect, and with an emphasis on making the death as painless and distress free as possible." Because "The AVMA does not take the death of nonhuman animals lightly…"[17]

How altogether sick is it that we live in a world where people are referred to as "pet parents" with "fur babies" that often get carried in a front pack made for a child, or pushed in a stroller, yet we kill our own kids in the womb? It's well and good to treat animals, especially our pets, well. Our family has a gigantic German Shepherd who seems to think that we are her staff and that our Arizona pool is her private resort, which is fine. But it's tragic that, if reincarnation was true (which it's not), some kids killed in the womb might come back to their family as a pet and actually be treated with decency.

The real issue under abortion is sex. The vast majority of abortions are single women who have sex outside of marriage. Some people will say that Christianity is the world's largest religion, but it is not. Sex is officially the world's largest religion with more passionate worshippers and evangelists than the Church, as we will learn in the next chapter.

2

SEX IS A RELIGION, LGBTQIA ARE DENOMINATIONS, AND ABORTION IS A DEMONIC COUNTERFEIT SACRIFICE

Ezekiel 16:20–21 (ESV) – ...you took your sons and your daughters, whom you had borne to me, and these you sacrificed to them to be devoured. Were your whorings so small a matter that you slaughtered my children and delivered them up as an offering by fire to them?

In Christianity, there are a variety of denominations that have their unique ways of Christian belief and practice. There are also sacraments or sacred acts, like baptism and communion, that publicly identify people with their religion so that others see and know of our religious commitment. Christianity is based on the concept of God the Father sending His Son, Jesus Christ, to bring us freedom. Christianity has evangelists and missionaries who devote their lives to encouraging others to convert to their religion. Lastly, Christian churches have children's ministry where the next generation is trained up to remain loyal to their religion.

Everything God creates Satan counterfeits. Paul says this very thing in Romans 1:18-32, "For the wrath of God is revealed from heaven against all ungodliness and unrighteousness of men, who by their unrighteousness suppress the truth...For although they knew God, they did not honor him as God or give thanks to him, but they became futile in their thinking, and their foolish hearts were darkened. Claiming to be wise, they became fools...Therefore God gave them up in the lusts of their hearts to impurity, to the dishonoring of their bodies among themselves, because they exchanged the truth about God for a lie and worshiped and served the creature rather than the Creator, who is blessed forever! Amen. For this reason God gave them up to dishonorable passions. For their women exchanged natural relations for those that are contrary to nature; and the men likewise gave up natural relations with women and were consumed with passion for one another, men committing shameless acts with men and receiving in themselves the due penalty for their error. And since they did not see fit to acknowledge God, God gave them up to a debased mind to do what ought not to be done. They were filled with all manner of unrighteousness, evil, covetousness, malice. They are full of envy, murder, strife, deceit, maliciousness. They are gossips, slanderers, haters of God, insolent, haughty, boastful, inventors of evil, disobedient to parents, foolish, faithless, heartless, ruthless. Though they know God's righteous decree that those who practice such things deserve to die, they not only do them but give approval to those who practice them."

    To summarize, if people do not worship the Creator, they wind up worshipping creation. Since the human body with its' passions and pleasures is the most beautiful and wonderful thing God made, we end up worshipping sex. We know that God has poured out His passive wrath when He allows people to do whatever they want, which only stores up wrath for the active day of wrath that awaits unrepentant sinners. People who worship the body and sex are foolish, but think they are wise. The counterfeit religion of sex has many different denominations and people act like missionaries and evangelists trying to convert people to join their sexual sacraments. When anyone speaks against people who worship sex as god, the truth is "suppressed" in everything from social media throttling to fake news and cancel culture. More recently, the religion of sex has decided that they need to have a children's ministry and, since their lifestyle does not produce many children, they have decided to take over schools and write curriculum to convert your kids to their religion.

LGBTQIA ARE DENOMINATIONS IN THE RELIGION OF SEX

Everything the Bible teaches about sex traces back to the first two chapters of Genesis, the book that opens with the famous words, "In the beginning...".[a] Human sexuality begins in the Garden of Eden, where God created all things good. He designed male, female, and sexuality. He defined gender, marriage, and sex as He meant it to be. We see the world as God made it and before sin corrupted it. When God told humans to "be fruitful and multiply",[b] He established marriage as a covenant to be consummated sexually. Moses recorded this, Jesus repeated it, and the apostle Paul echoed it. Long before human governments existed, God created marriage and established the family unit as the first building block of cultures and nations.

If Genesis 1-2 presents the world as God meant it to be, Genesis 3 reports the human race's terrible leap into sin. Tragically, sex and marriage were among the first casualties, as the rest of Genesis reports. We see not only the triumph of love and romantic commitment[c] but also the disaster of polygamy[d] and a slew of heartbreaking love triangles.[e] In the days of Noah, many defied God's ban on marriage between believers and unbelievers.[f] A mismatched marriage causes grief that reaches to extended family.[g] There are also sad accounts of a loveless marriage[h] and the pain of divorce.[i]

The Old Testament records endless episodes of sexual sin and its consequences. Examples of broken sexuality include rampant lust in Sodom,[j] the womanizing of a key spiritual leader,[k] the sexual failings of great kings,[l] and incestuous rape.[m]

Sex is now the official religion of western culture and much

---

[a]Gen. 1:1 [b]Gen.1:28 [c]Gen. 24:1–67, 29:20 [d]Gen. 4:18–24, 28:46–49, 29:14–29 [e]Gen. 16:1–16, 29:31–30:24 [f]Gen. 6:1–2 [g]Gen. 26:34–35 [h]Gen. 29:31 [i]Gen. 21:8–14, 23:1–2, 25:1 [j]Gen. 19 [k]-see Samson, Judges 16 [l]see David and Bathsheba, 2 Samuel 11–12; plus Solomon's many wives, 1 Kings 11:1–6 [m]see Amnon's rape of Tamar, 2 Samuel 13:1–22

bigger than Christianity. Easter and Christmas get a few days, but "Pride" gets an entire month. You cannot pray in a public school, but you can come out of the closet to the praise of your teachers and classmates. LGBTQIA are denominations in the religion of sex. A teacher or administrator can get in a lot of trouble carrying a Bible to class, but not if they wear a rainbow sweatshirt. This is even though the Bible says that a rainbow is God, as a warrior, hanging His bow in the sky, promising to never flood the earth again as He did in judging sinners by water in the days of Noah. Each denomination in the religion of sex is at odds with the Bible, which lists sexual acts outside of monogamous heterosexual marriage, including the following sexual acts, as forbidden for God's people:

1. Fornication[a]
2. Adultery[b]
3. Polygamy[c]
4. Rape[d]
5. Incest[e]
6. Homosexuality[f]
7. Bestiality[g]
8. Prostitution[h]
9. Sexual Immorality ["porneia"][i]

[a]Gen. 38:24; cf. Lev. 21:9; Deut. 22:21; 1 Cor. 6:18, 7:2; Heb. 13:4 [b]Ex. 20:14; Deut. 5:18; Prov. 6:32; Matt. 5:27-32, 15:19; 1 Cor. 6:9-11 [c]Gen. 2:1-8 cf. Matt. 19:4-6; Gen. 4:19-24; 1 Ki. 11:1-9; 1 Tim. 3:2,12 [d]Gen. 34:1-31; Jdg. 19:1-30, 2 Sam. 13:11-14 [e]Lev. 18, 20, 27 [f]Lev. 18:22, 20:13; Rom. 1:26-27; 1 Cor. 6:9 [g]Ex. 22:19; Lev. 20:15-16; Deut. 27:21 [h]Lev. 19:29; 21:9; 1 Cor. 6:16 [i]Matt. 19:9; 1 Cor. 6:13, 6:18; Eph. 5:3; 1 Thess. 4:3

10. Pagan sexual activity[a]

Notice that the Bible is restrictive on many kinds of sexual activity, and no one sexual activity is singled out. Far more items concern heterosexual boundaries than other sexual sins.

According to the Bible, sex does not merely involve our bodies, it also includes our souls.[b] The Bible takes a very positive view of sex within heterosexual marriage (e.g. Song of Songs), and a very negative view when sex is removed from God's design for marriage. The fiery passions of sex are designed by God to be safely kept in the hearth of marriage to warm the home and, when taken out of their intended place, homes, families, generations, and nations are burned to the ground. This is precisely what is happening as we worship sex and sacrifice our children as, according to one study, 49% of people who got an abortion used it as their only form of birth control and were not even making any attempt to not get pregnant.[18]

WHEN SEX IS A DEMONIC RELIGION, DEAD CHILDREN ARE THE SACRIFICE

When sex is a demonic religion, dead children are the sacrifice. The sacrifice of one's child is the demonic counterfeit of the death of the Son of God for our sins. This demonic activity is nothing new and is common throughout the Old Testament.

Solomon's wives practiced other false demonic religions and eventually the same man who built the Temple for the Lord also built places for the worship of demons. Solomon worshipped demonic false gods with his many wives, had forbidden sex that likely extended beyond his 700 wives and 300 concubines, encouraged others including God's people to do the same, and paid for the

---

[a]Ex. 32, Is. 57:7-8, Hosea 4:12-14, Eph. 5:5, Col. 3:5 [b]e.g. 1 Corinthians 6:15-16

equivalent of a one-stop shop cult/strip club/abortion clinic that he received from God's people through the tithe.

Ashtoreth (also known as Venus) is the Canaanite goddess of sex often worshipped with her male counterpart Baal with sex being part of their cultic worship. Just like our day that has landmarks, icons, and signs to let people know where churches and businesses are, this sex cult had large poles put in the ground atop high places as phallic symbols to let everyone know where to go to find the most sinister sex. She was one of many ancient demons considered the "holy ones" or sacred prostitutes and idols representing her were often nude and pornographic.

Milcom (also known as Molech) was the demonic chief god of the ancient Ammonites, and the Bible mocks him as the Hebrew equivalent of his name is "shame". After Solomon's father conquered the Ammonites and their demons in battle by the power of Yahweh, they, "took the crown of Milcom from his head; the weight of it was a talent of gold (roughly 70 pounds), and in it was a precious stone; and it was placed on David's head".[a] Solomon worshipping this demon god is a complete betrayal of both his God and father along with the Kingdom he inherited from both. A Bible dictionary says, "Worship of this deity, which was accompanied by sacrificing children in the fire, was strictly prohibited to Israel (Lev 18:21; Jer 32:35). Solomon built Milcom a worship site (1 Kgs 11:5, 33), which Josiah later tore down along with other sites built by Solomon in worship to demons (2 Kgs 23:13)."[19]

Their counterfeit worship of Molech involved both sex and the sacrifice of children, including firstborn sons as a mockery of Jesus Christ the firstborn Son of God who died to save sinners.[b] They even sacrificed their own children by fire as if they were placing them on the flames of hell.[c] Even Mesha, the king of Moab, sacrificed

---

[a]2 Samuel 12:30; 1 Chronicles 20:2, NRSV [b]Leviticus 18:21; 20:2-5; 2 Kings 23:10; Jeremiah 32:35 [c]2 Chronicles 33:6; 2 Kings 16:3; 21:6

his firstborn son as a burnt offering to Molech.[a] Molech was such a powerful demonic force that it seduced many of God's people into sexual sin, "whoring after Molech".[b]

Chemosh is the ancient demon god worshipped by the Moabites as their national deity, which are the people Ruth was saved from. Scholars believe that the female counterpart of Chemosh was the demon goddess Ishtar (also called Astar, or the Mother Goddess). This demon god and demon goddess were said to have an intense and perverted sexual relationship and were to be worshipped in sanctuaries that were counterfeits of the Temple that Solomon built for the worship of Yahweh. Because everything God creates, Satan counterfeits, they also had pagan priests whose duties included overseeing the sexual orgies at the temple, and not only sacrificing animals but also children to the demon gods of sex.[c] The cult/strip club/abortion clinic that Solomon built was destroyed and was judged by God as purely evil, despite being popular and profitable.[d]

One academic Bible resource summarizes ancient infanticide saying, "Child sacrifice was an important part of Phoenician religion. A large cemetery dating to 400–200 bc in the Phoenician city of Carthage contained 20,000 urns with the cremated remains of 20,000–40,000 children as old as four. The inscriptions at the site indicate that the children were sacrificed to a Phoenician god, though the reason for the sacrifice is unclear. The biblical text indicates that King Mesha of neighboring Moab sacrificed his son to Chemosh in an attempt to avert defeat at the hands of the Israelites (2 Kgs 3:26–27). Other texts suggest that Israelites may have also sacrificed their children to Molech, the deity of their Ammonite neighbors (Lev 18:21; 20:2–5; 2 Kgs 23:10; Jer 7:31; 32:35)."[20]

We are battling the same demons today, and they want to do to the marriage of Christians what they did to the marriage of Solomon and Abishag. We must never forget that Satan did not even show up

[a]2 Kings 3:26-27 [b]Leviticus 20:5 [c]2 Kings 3:27 [d]2 Kings 23:13

and attack our first parents, Adam and Eve, until after their wedding. In another book we wrote on spiritual warfare called "Win Your War", we emphasized that, according to the Bible, after the wedding comes the war and spiritual warfare starts in your marriage. This truth is tragically and grossly on display in the sinful sex of Solomon. He serves as a sobering and frightening example of what any one of us is capable of if we take our sin and our God too lightly. If you have already started down the same path of destruction, the longer you wait, the darker, grosser, and deadlier each step becomes. Today is the day for you to turn around, which is repentance, and run to God for forgiveness and restoration.

If you claim to be a Christian and are disagreeing with the pro-life position, you need to be aware that Christianity did not start with you, is not defined by you, and will not be edited for you. To be adopted by God our Father is to be included in His family, the Church. As we will learn next, God has determined that life begins at conception and science confirms this fact.

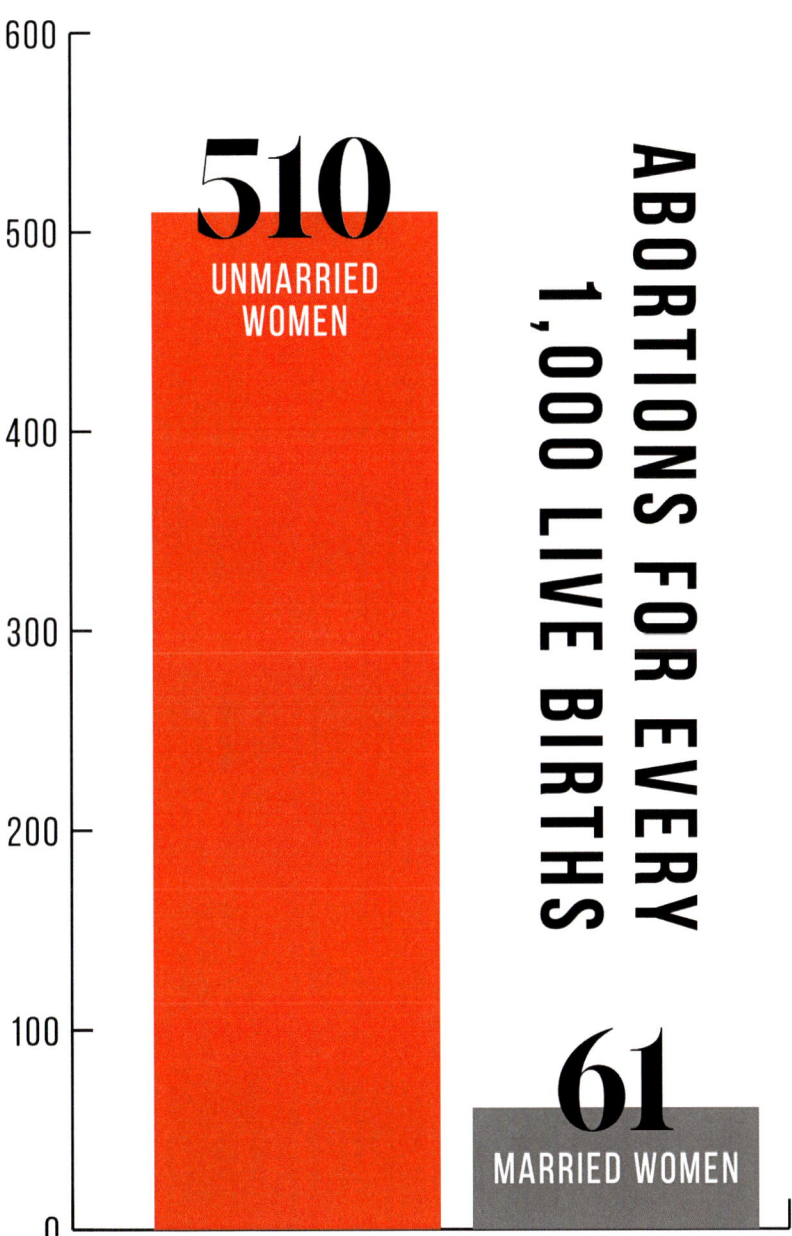

ROUGHLY 1 IN 5 PREGNANCIES THAT DON'T END IN MISCARRIAGE, DO END IN ABORTION.

MEDICATION ABORTIONS ACCOUNT FOR ROUGHLY 4 IN 10 ABORTIONS.

ROUGHLY 6 IN 10 ABORTIONS ARE BY WOMEN WITH ONE OR MORE CHILDREN.

3

FOLLOW THE SCIENCE...
LIFE BEGINS AT CONCEPTION

Psalm 139:13-14 (CEB) — You are the one who created my innermost parts; you knit me together while I was still in my mother's womb. I give thanks to you that I was marvelously set apart. Your works are wonderful—I know that very well.

When my wife Grace was pregnant with each of our five children, at some point in the pregnancy, we had the big day of going into the doctor's office for the ultrasound. I would hold her hand as we watched the monitor show us the baby. It was amazing to see into the womb and see what God has always seen. The medical technician would stop and show us the hands and fingers, toes and feet, head, and mouth, and let us know if we were having a boy or a girl. Perhaps most amazing, we would then get to hear the heartbeat. Simply seeing our unborn baby made it abundantly clear to us that growing in the womb of my best friend was a human life.

As we had more and more children, the ultrasound technology got better and better. By the birth of our fifth child, it was like going from old black and white grainy television footage to color television. Today, an ultrasound is like watching high-definition television. The intricate details of growing human life in the womb are clearer and more compelling than ever.

This leads to an old but important question: When does life begin? Because human beings have rights, if the unborn child is a person, then they have a right to not have their life taken. Therefore, this question is incredibly significant.

WHEN DOES HUMAN LIFE BEGIN?

Scientifically and medically, it is beyond debate that human life begins at conception. From the initial joining of sperm and egg, the tiny baby is alive, distinct from its mother, and living and growing as a human being.[21]

The unified determination of the scientific and medical community is as follows, "The zygote is composed of human DNA and other human molecules, so its nature is undeniably human and not some other species. This DNA includes a complete 'design,' guiding not only early development but even hereditary attributes that will appear in childhood and adulthood, from hair, sex, and eye color to personality traits….The new human zygote has a genetic composition that is absolutely unique to itself, different from any other human that has ever existed, including that of its mother (thus disproving the claim that what is involved in abortion is merely 'a woman and her body')…It is also quite clear that the earliest human embryo is biologically alive. It fulfills the four criteria needed to establish biological life: metabolism, growth, reaction to stimuli, and reproduction…Finally, is the human zygote merely a new kind of cell or is it a human organism; that is, a human being? Scientists define an organism as a complex structure of interdependent elements constituted to carry on the activities of life by separately-functioning but mutually dependent organs…The human zygote meets this definition with ease. Once formed, it initiates a complex sequence of events to ready it for continued development and growth: The zygote acts immediately and decisively to initiate a program of development that will, if uninterrupted by accident, disease, or external intervention, proceed seamlessly through formation of the definitive body, birth, childhood, adolescence, maturity, and aging, ending with death. This coordinated behavior is the very hallmark of an organism."[22]

While the ability to express humanity and personhood changes throughout the life cycle, human essence and human personhood are innate to the living being. No matter how tiny or weak, humans deserve support and protection because they are God's image bearers. Princeton professor and former member of the President's Council on Bioethics, Robert P. George, says, "Human embryos are not...some other type of animal organism, like a dog or cat. Neither are they a part of an organism, like a heart, a kidney, or a skin cell. Nor again are they a disorganized aggregate, a mere clump of cells awaiting some magical transformation. Rather, a human embryo is a whole living member of the species Homo sapiens in the earliest stage of his or her natural development. Unless severely damaged, or denied or deprived of a suitable environment, a human being in the embryonic stage will, by directing its own integral organic functioning, develop himself or herself to the next more mature developmental stage, i.e., the fetal stage. The embryonic, fetal, child, and adolescent stages are stages in the development of a determinate and enduring entity—a human being—who comes into existence as a single-celled organism (the zygote) and develops, if all goes well, into adulthood many years later. But does this mean that the human embryo is a human person worthy of full moral respect? Must the early embryo never be used as a mere means for the benefit of others simply because it is a human being? The answer...is 'Yes.'"[23]

Roe v Wade legalized abortion in the United States on January 22, 1973. However, it was widely known prior to this landmark decision that life begins at conception. The decision was not so much medical, but rather political.

In his classic work, *Development Anatomy: A Textbook and Laboratory Manual of Embryology*, published in 1965, L.B. Arey says, "By the time a baby is eighteen to twenty-five days old, long before the mother is sure that she is pregnant, the heart is already beating. At forty-five days after conception, you can pick up electroencephalographic waves from the baby's developing brain. At eight weeks, there is a brain. By the ninth and tenth weeks, the thyroid and the adrenal glands are functioning. The baby can squint, swallow, move his tongue and the sex hormones are already present. By twelve weeks the fingerprints on the hands have already formed and except for size, will never change. At thirteen weeks, he has fingernails, he sucks his thumb, and he can recoil from pain."[24]

In addition, Arey says, "In the fourth month the growing baby is eight to ten inches long. In the fifth month there is a time of lengthening and strengthening of the developing infant. Skin, hair, and nails grow. Sweat glands arise. Oil glands excrete. This is the month in which the movements of the infant are felt by his mother. In the sixth month the developing baby responds to light and to sound. He can sleep and awake. He gets hiccups and can hear the beat of his mother's heart. Survival outside the womb is now possible. In the seventh month the nervous system becomes much more complex, the infant is sixteen inches long and weighs about three pounds. In the eighth and ninth months there is a time of fattening and of continued growth."[25]

In summary, there is no reasonable conclusion if the medical science is followed to come to any conclusion other than the fact that life begins at conception.

15 MEDICAL PROOFS THAT LIFE BEGINS AT CONCEPTION

In a lengthy article published by Princeton, there is a list of quotes that all illustrate and reinforce the fact that the starting point for a human life occurs with the formation of the one-celled zygote. These powerful medical quotes are reported below without edit:[26]

1. "Development of the embryo begins at Stage 1 when a sperm

fertilizes an oocyte and together they form a zygote."[27]

2. "Human development begins after the union of male and female gametes or germ cells during a process known as fertilization (conception)...Fertilization is a sequence of events that begins with the contact of a sperm (spermatozoon) with a secondary oocyte (ovum) and ends with the fusion of their pronuclei (the haploid nuclei of the sperm and ovum) and the mingling of their chromosomes to form a new cell. This fertilized ovum, known as a zygote, is a large diploid cell that is the beginning, or primordium, of a human being."[28]

3. "Embryo: the developing organism from the time of fertilization until significant differentiation has occurred, when the organism becomes known as a fetus."[29]

4. "Embryo: An organism in the earliest stage of development; in a man, from the time of conception to the end of the second month in the uterus."[30]

5. "Embryo: The early developing fertilized egg that is growing into another individual of the species. In man the term 'embryo' is usually restricted to the period of development from fertilization until the end of the eighth week of pregnancy."[31]

6. "The development of a human being begins with fertilization, a process by which two highly specialized cells, the spermatozoon from the male and the oocyte from the female, unite to give rise to a new organism, the zygote."[32]

7. "Embryo: The developing individual between the union of the germ cells and the completion of the organs which characterize its body when it becomes a separate organism...At the moment the sperm cell of the human male meets the ovum of the female and the union results in a fertilized ovum (zygote), a new life has begun...The term embryo covers the several stages of early development from conception to the ninth or tenth week of life."[33]

8. "I would say that among most scientists, the word 'embryo'

includes the time from after fertilization…"[34]

9. "The development of a human begins with fertilization, a process by which the spermatozoon from the male and the oocyte from the female unite to give rise to a new organism, the zygote."[35]

10. "The question came up of what is an embryo, when does an embryo exist, when does it occur. I think, as you know, that in development, life is a continuum…But I think one of the useful definitions that has come out, especially from Germany, has been the stage at which these two nuclei [from sperm and egg] come together and the membranes between the two break down."[36]

11. "Zygote. This cell, formed by the union of an ovum and a sperm (Gr. zygtos, yoked together), represents the beginning of a human being. The common expression 'fertilized ovum' refers to the zygote."[37]

12. "The chromosomes of the oocyte and sperm are…respectively enclosed within female and male pronuclei. These pronuclei fuse with each other to produce the single, diploid, 2N nucleus of the fertilized zygote. This moment of zygote formation may be taken as the beginning or zero time point of embryonic development."[38]

13. "Although life is a continuous process, fertilization is a critical landmark because, under ordinary circumstances, a new, genetically distinct human organism is thereby formed…The combination of 23 chromosomes present in each pronucleus results in 46 chromosomes in the zygote. Thus the diploid number is restored and the embryonic genome is formed. The embryo now exists as a genetic unity."[39]

14. "Almost all higher animals start their lives from a single cell, the fertilized ovum (zygote)…The time of fertilization represents the starting point in the life history, or ontogeny, of the individual."[40]

15. "[A]nimal biologists use the term embryo to describe the single cell stage, the two-cell stage, and all subsequent stages up until a time when recognizable humanlike limbs and facial features

begin to appear between six to eight weeks after fertilization...[A] number of specialists working in the field of human reproduction have suggested that we stop using the word embryo to describe the developing entity that exists for the first two weeks after fertilization. In its place, they proposed the term pre-embryo...I'll let you in on a secret. The term pre-embryo has been embraced wholeheartedly by IVF practitioners for reasons that are political, not scientific. The new term is used to provide the illusion that there is something profoundly different between what we nonmedical biologists still call a six-day-old embryo and what we and everyone else call a sixteen-day-old embryo...The term pre-embryo is useful in the political arena -- where decisions are made about whether to allow early embryo (now called pre-embryo) experimentation -- as well as in the confines of a doctor's office, where it can be used to allay moral concerns that might be expressed by IVF patients. 'Don't worry,' a doctor might say, 'it's only pre-embryos that we're manipulating or freezing. They won't turn into real human embryos until after we've put them back into your body.'"[41]

In summary, Professor Emeritus of Human Embryology of the University of Arizona School of Medicine, Dr. C. Ward Kischer affirms the fact that life begins at conception.[42] Dr. Kischer affirms that "Every human embryologist, worldwide, states that the life of the new individual human being begins at fertilization (conception)."[43] He goes on to say, "Even authors who philosophically lean towards not attributing the same value to human life at the one-cell stage as they do to later stages of development admit that 'As far as human "life" per se, it is, for the most part, uncontroversial among the scientific and philosophical community that life begins at the moment when the genetic information contained in the sperm and ovum combine to form a genetically unique cell.'"[44] Lastly, J.T. Eberl goes on to focus on the heart of the debate which is political and not medical saying, "However, what is controversial is whether this genetically unique cell should be considered a human person."[45]

The entire misguided debate of when human life begins is driven by a profoundly Western bias. In many Eastern cultures a child is counted as one year old at birth, because their life began in the womb prior to their birth. Cultures who have used this alternative age system that honors unborn life as truly life include the Japanese and the Buddhist religion, South Koreans, Chinese, as well as in Taiwan, Hong Kong, and Vietnam.

ABORTION IS A POLITICAL ISSUE NOT ROOTED IN MEDICAL OR LEGAL RATIONALE

The issue of when life begins is abundantly clear, medically and scientifically. Furthermore, legally, this is an established fact under various state laws on "fetal homicide and penalty" that are "crimes against pregnant women".[46] There are laws in various states regarding "fetal homicide" pertaining to the killing of an unborn baby by violent acts against the pregnant mother. Currently, at least 38 states have fetal homicide laws, and at least 29 states have fetal homicide laws that apply to the earliest stages of pregnancy.[47] Simply stated, if someone commits a violent act against a pregnant woman that causes the termination of her pregnancy, in most states, that would be considered a crime and even murder because an innocent unborn life has been taken.

Furthermore, there are cases where the neglect of a pregnant woman for her unborn baby have led to legal charges against the mother for such things as extreme drug use while pregnant that damaged the health of her growing baby. For example, in the case of Whitner v. State of South Carolina, the South Carolina Supreme Court determined that a viable fetus was a "person" with legal rights under the Children's Code and could be the victim of criminal neglect just like a birthed child could be.⁴⁸ The case is a tragic one as the 28-year-old mother had a serious drug addiction, was using crack cocaine throughout her pregnancy and gave birth to a son with cocaine residue in his system. The mother was convicted and imprisoned for child abuse. Admittedly, the woman's addiction is devastating, and she needs healing and deliverance from her addiction. However, she did put cocaine in the body of her baby and the same child with drugs in their system lived inside and outside of the womb as she was abusing her child. The mother freely chose what happened to her unborn baby, and it was a crime. Had she chosen an abortion pill instead of cocaine, she would have not committed a crime but instead been extolled for exercising her right.

Additionally, there are numerous medical procedures performed on an unborn child in their mother's womb to preserve their life which simply reinforces the truth that an unborn baby is a living human being. Johns Hopkins reports that, for unborn children who are patients, they can do such things as heart repair, various surgeries, spina bifida repair, transfusion, lung repair, and laser surgery, among other procedures, to aid the health of a growing baby in the womb.⁴⁹

The issue of abortion is not much of a medical or scientific issue, but rather political. Shortly after a draft opinion by the U.S. Supreme Court was leaked that indicated that Roe v Wade may be overturned, 49 Democrats voted in support of the Women's Health Protection Act of 2022 that supported abortion up to birth nationwide.⁵⁰ That brutal bill defined childhood liability as follows, "The term 'viability' means the point in a pregnancy at which, in the good-faith medical judgment of the treating health care provider, based on the particular facts of the case before the health care provider, there is a reasonable likelihood of sustained fetal survival outside the uterus with or without artificial support."⁵¹

It is commonly accepted that fetal viability, the ability of the child to live outside of their mother's womb, is somewhere between 20 and 23 weeks.[52] Most everyone knows someone who was a "premie" born weeks or months before their due date. To allow the ending of a healthy human life is simply infanticide. Some extreme abortion advocates admit this is their agenda. It is hard to know how many babies born alive are killed outside of the womb, since only six states require reporting on abortions that result in the baby being born alive (Arizona, Florida, Michigan, Minnesota, Oklahoma, Texas).[53] For example, "In Stenberg v. Carhart,\1\...the United States Supreme Court struck down a Nebraska law banning partial-birth abortion, a procedure in which an abortionist delivers an unborn child's body until only the head remains inside of the womb, punctures the back of the child's skull with scissors, and sucks the child's brains out before completing the delivery...The Carhart Court considered the location of an infant's body at the moment of death during a partial-birth abortion--delivered partly outside the

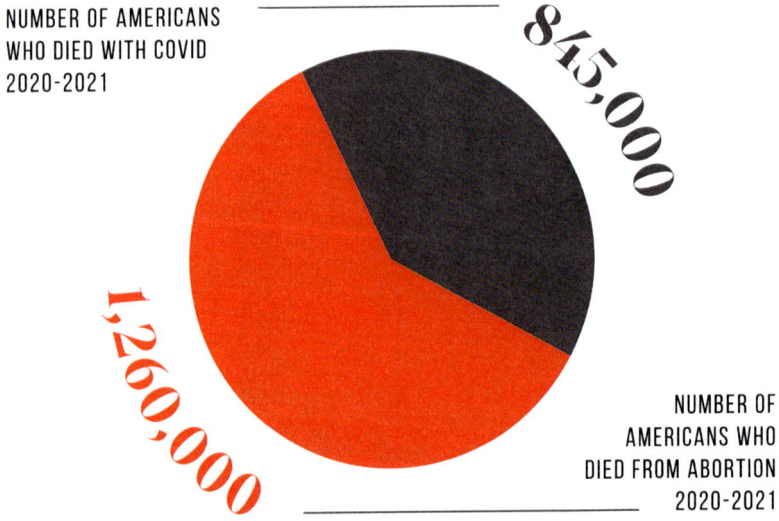

cdc.gov, guttmacher.org

body of the mother--to be of no legal significance in ruling on the constitutionality of the Nebraska law. Instead, implicit in the Carhart decision was the pernicious notion that a partially-born infant's entitlement to the protections of the law is dependent upon whether or not the partially-born child's mother wants him or her."[54]

Less than a month after the vote on the Women's Health Protection Act of 2022 to extend abortion to the time of birth, the city of New York kept in place a mask mandate requiring children five and under to wear a mask in preschools and care centers to protect against COVID-19.[55] Globally, only .4% of people who died with COVID-19 (not of COVID-19) were children, which means that we celebrate killing a viable child but, if they are born, we need to cover them with a mask because they are too precious to risk even possibly getting a flu that will likely not kill them.[56] These are all irrational political conclusions and not rational medical or scientific decisions.

There are also frequent news stories of babies born very prematurely that lived and were viable for life. For example, in April 2021, Curtis Means was discharged after 275 days in the University of

Curtis Means, 2021

Alabama at Birmingham Regional Neonatal Intensive Care Unit. He was born at just 21 weeks and one day of gestation and was entered in the Guinness Book of World Records as the most premature baby to survive, having been born 132 days premature.[57]

Having established the medical fact that life begins at conception, and that an unborn baby is a human being worthy of legal rights, we will now examine why human life is uniquely sacred compared to other life forms, such as plants and animals.

4
HUMAN LIFE IS UNIQUELY SACRED

Genesis 1:27 (ESV) – …God created man in his own image, in the image of God he created him; male and female he created them.

In the last few years, the news has been repeatedly filled with angry people in the streets demanding justice for those killed by police officers (which seems pro-life), the shutting down of businesses and churches for COVID-19 (which seems pro-life), and the demanding of abortion to kill babies (which seems pro-death). There is an obvious bias ageist discrimination going on by born people who are prejudiced against unborn people and suffering from "unbornophobia".

Ours is a strange world. On one hand, people believe that human beings are highly evolved animals – the byproduct of the fittest surviving by dominating and overtaking the weaker and less fit. On the other hand, people also believe that human beings are invaluable – worthy of justice, equality, and compensation for any perceived wrong they may have endured from those who used power in a way that evolutionary thought celebrates. If human beings are nothing more than highly evolved animals, then we should be no more surprised that someone uses their power to harm a weaker person than be shocked when a lion chases down a gazelle and eats it, or expect the gazelle's family to hold a press conference with their attorney demanding justice and compensation for the less fit. We are not animals, which explains why we feel outraged when people act like animals, no matter how many times we are wrongly told that we are animals.

If we believe in mercy and justice for those who are lacking power, what about the unborn who are most powerless? If we believe in rights for women, what about the unborn women who are being killed daily? If we believe that lives matter, what about unborn lives?

ONLY THE BIBLE TEACHES THAT HUMAN LIFE IS SACRED AND EQUAL

Despite all the indoctrination that subversively passes as education, there remains in human beings, because of the conscience God gave us, an innate sense that human life matters. This idea of equality did not pop into existence like a cartoon thought bubble. History shows where equality as a value and way of life did or did not emerge. And a pair of surprising forces have been no friends of equality. World religions did not come up with the idea of equal rights. Nor did it originate in a secular, non-religious outlook.

No major faith apart from Christianity mandates a deep commitment to the equality of all people. In every other religion, certain individuals and classes rank higher than others on a ladder of spiritual attainment. They are more enlightened, more holy, further along in paying their karmic debt, closer to the divine by virtue of their good works, and so on. And the result can be horrific inequities. In Hindu culture, for example, the caste system made untold masses unequal and untouchable. In Muslim culture, sharia law gives women and outsiders nothing resembling the rights and privileges of the male faithful.

When you ask yourself, "Do the religions of the world contribute to equality?", the honest answer is no. The idea of equality of all people likewise did not originate in a non-religious belief system. The foundation of a dominant secular worldview, evolution, leads to the conclusion that some are more fit than others. Some deserve to be winners and losers deserve to die. And by placing animals and human beings on a continuum of development, evolution has given rise to racist views that some individuals, peoples, and races are more advanced than others. In our debate on ABC Nightline, Deepak Chopra, for example, referred to me and some other people as "primitive".

Taken to its logical end, an unadulterated evolutionary view of humanity cannot lead to equality. In fact, only the Bible provides reasoning for the equality of human beings. This fact is why the preamble to the American Declaration of Independence begins, "We hold these truths to be self-evident, that all men are created equal, that they are endowed by their Creator with certain unalienable Rights…" Equality and rights come from God, not the government. God made us, and He says we have value no matter what the government might say. It does not matter your age, race, class, religious beliefs, sexual orientation, intelligence, power, or income – you are valuable, not because of what you have or do but because God made you!

The equality of all human beings is a biblical idea that has made a powerful impact far beyond the walls of church. It has touched societies around the globe and been adopted even by our most vocal opponents. Scholar Nancy Pearcey points out that none other than the eminent atheist Friedrich Nietzsche gave Christianity credit for the concept of equality. In *The Will to Power*, he wrote, "Another Christian concept…has passed even more deeply into the tissue of modernity: the concept of the 'equality of souls before God.' This concept furnishes the prototype of all theories of equal rights." Pearcey cites the postmodernist Richard Rorty as another radical atheist who admits that "the idea of universal human rights was a completely novel concept in history, resting on the biblical teaching 'that all human beings are created in the image of God.'" Pearcey comments: "Rorty admits that atheists like himself have no basis for human rights within their own worldview. He calls himself a 'freeloading atheist' because he is fully aware that he is borrowing the idea of rights and human dignity from the Christian heritage."[58]

IMAGE AND LIKENESS

Who do you think you are? Where do we even start to answer that enormous question? Let's start at the beginning. You are an image bearer of God.

Genesis, the book of beginnings, 1:26-27 reports, "God said, 'Let us make man in our image, after our likeness. And let them have dominion over the fish of the sea and over the birds of the heavens and over the livestock and over all the earth and over every creeping thing that creeps on the earth.' So God created man in his own image, in the image of God he created him; male and female he created them."

The Trinitarian God, who lives in eternal friendship, created us to image Him. God uniquely honors humanity in this way. He's made nothing else in His image. Animals and plants do not bear God's image. This honor is distinctively reserved by God for human life. Practically, this means that God made us to image, or reflect Him, as a mirror does. And in a world where we're encouraged to spend much time gazing at ourselves in a mirror, it's helpful every time we look in the mirror to be reminded that we're made to mirror God to others. He created us to reflect His goodness and glory in the world around us, like Moses, who radiated the glory of God after being in God's presence.[a] You were created by God, are on the earth to image and glorify God, and when you die, if you are in Christ, you will be

---

[a]*Exodus 34:30*

with God forever, imaging and glorifying Him perfectly in a sinless state.

The question of identity is one that humans have struggled with since Satan's conversation with our first parents. Only by seeing ourselves rightly and biblically between God and the animals can we have both humility and dignity. There alone are we as God intended us to be. By understanding our position under God as created beings, we should remain humble toward and dependent upon God. By understanding our position of dominion over creation, we embrace our dignity as morally superior to animals.

The Bible states plainly and repeatedly that we come from God, we are under the authority of God, and, in the end, we will be judged by God. There are 12 vital truths revealed in the fact that we were made in the image and likeness of God. Taken together, they provide the essence of a biblical anthropology, or view of humanity from God's intention as our Creator, that has massive implications for virtually every discipline from anthropology to sociology, politics, and philosophy.

1. We were created by the Trinity. Augustine was fond of noting that the plural language of Genesis 1:26, "Let us make man in our image, after our likeness," means we were created by the Trinity. We are to understand ourselves not as autonomous individuals but rather as image bearers made for four categories of relationship. Theologically, we are to live in relationship with God. Psychologically, we are to live in relationship with ourselves, knowing who God intends for us to be. Socially, we are to live in relationship with other people, in community. Environmentally, we are to live in relationship with all that God has put under our dominion, including animals.
2. We were created as persons by a personal God. Unlike the rest of creation, which was made solely by God's word, God formed us

by his proverbial hands and then breathed life into us to speak to us.[a]

3. God originally made mankind without sin. Genesis 1:31 calls our first parents "very good" in comparison to the rest of creation, which God simply called "good". Ecclesiastes 7:29 says, "God made man upright." Therefore, all human sin is fully the responsibility of sinners and not of God our Creator. In addition, all the effects of sin and the curse were not originally part of the world God created for us in love.

4. God blesses us.[b] God is good and does not need to be prompted or compelled to give grace; rather, He delights in doing so and does so without request.

5. Unlike the animals who were made according to their "own kind," we are made in the "image of God." Human life is distinct from and superior to all other created things. We are altogether unique with special dignity, value, and worth.

6. God gives commands to us because He made us as moral image bearers. We can know right and wrong and we can respond to God with moral obedience as an act of faith in love.

7. God made us curious adventurers and granted us permission to explore His creation through everything from a telescope to a microscope.[c] We have an insatiable curiosity that begins at birth and continues throughout life as we seek to experience and learn, travel the world, and explore every nook of creation.

8. God created us to be creative and make culture.[d] This explains the innate love people have for everything from fashion to film, music, theater, architecture, painting, photography, dance, and storytelling.

9. God created us to be reproductive and have children.[e] This explains why people long to be parents and consider children a great blessing.

[a]*Genesis 2:7* [b]*Genesis 1:28* [c]*Ibid* [d]*Ibid, 40* [e]*Ibid, 40*

10. God made us with meaningful work to do.[a] This explains why there is an innate drive in most people to work.
11. God created us as His image bearers, but not because He needed us in any way. He bestowed on us the dignity of being His image bearers solely for our benefit, not His own. God needs us for nothing but gives us everything like a loving Father who generously cares for His kids.
12. God created us to live coram Deo, "before the face of God" as friends. This Latin phase was commonly used by theologians throughout church history to explain the Christian life. Practically speaking, we were created to live all of life in the presence of God, under the authority of God, according to the Word of God, by the power of God, to the glory of God. Nothing in our life is secular or separated from the sight of God because all of life is sacred.

After God created our first parents in His image and likeness, they, unlike the rest of creation, related to God in a unique way. For starters, mankind was not made to live independent of God but rather dependent upon God. Human beings are created by God, spoken to in commands by God, and expected to live in relationship with and obedience to God.

Like a child is dependent upon a parent to care for them and speak to them, so is our relationship with God from the Garden. We were given the ability to communicate with God and one another that no other creature was given. We can hear God's Word and live in light of revelation from Him. Even in their sinless state, our first parents were dependent upon God, needed to hear from Him, and be in His presence. Thus, in our sinful and fallen state, we even more desperately need to hear from and be with God. Thankfully, this is possible because, unlike lower creation, such as plants and animals,

[a]*Genesis 2:15-17*

our relationship with God is tethered with words – He speaks to us through Scripture and other forms of revelation, and we speak to Him in such things as prayer and song.

As thinking beings, we can interpret and make meaning out of the revelation we receive. Simply, we can think, ponder, consider, probe, and learn unlike anything else God has made. For us to correctly understand and apply the revelation we receive, we must seek to love God with all our mind so that the facts we receive can be not just mental information, but information that contributes to our moral transformation.

As worshipers, revelation and interpretation culminate in exaltation. Because they were image bearers, our first parents were created to worship God in thought, word, deed, and motive. All their life was supposed to be lived in light of who God is, what God does, and what God says. They were supposed to interpret all this revelation and respond to God in ways that would both bring Him glory and them joy as they were doing what He created them to do.

THE 3 COMMON WAYS WE ERROR IN SEEING HUMAN LIFE

There are, generally speaking, three broad categories of Christian errors regarding the doctrine of image. The first is not maintaining the rightful place of humanity in God's created order. The second is reductionism that seeks to make one part of our humanity the defining aspect of what it means to be human. The third is defining what it means to be God's image bearers in terms of something we do rather than who we are. We will deal with each category of error in succession.

First, error occurs regarding the doctrine of image when there is a failure to maintain the theological tension that Scripture does. Genesis 1 and 2 (especially 1:26) reveals that mankind was made under God in and over the rest of creation. Generally speaking, nearly every error in anthropology puts us up to be divine like God or pushes us down to be animals like the rest of creation.

The former is common when human sinfulness is overlooked and/or there is an erroneous belief that we are somehow part of the divine, common in pantheism and panentheism, as if we had at least a spark of divinity within us. This is the view of Margaret Sanger who founded birth control as you will learn in chapter 8.

The latter is common when humans are seen as little more than highly evolved animals who should follow our desires for power and indulgence. This explains why, for example, such things as sexual sin are celebrated in our culture. If we are little more than animals with no moral compass above our instinctual drives, then we should act like animals and not feel bad about it. We do well to dominate and cancel others and satisfy every passion. This explains everything from gluttony to sexual perversion and commitment to radical environmentalism, and animal rights activism placing humanity at or near the same level of plants and animals. Extreme examples of this error include the occasional legal efforts to extend human rights to animals by the same people who deny the rights of the unborn.

Second, numerous errors emerge when it is believed that, rather than being God's image bearers in total, we bear the image of God in some specific part of us. This is called the substantive view and has been the predominant position historically. One theologian writes that, in this mode of thought, the imago Dei refers to "something within the substantial form of human nature, some faculty or capacity man possesses" that distinguishes "man from nature and from other animals".[59]

The truth is that it is not just a part of us that bears God's image while the rest of us does not. Instead, we are in totality (mind, body, soul, etc.) the image of God. When a part of us is thought to be the image of God, or at least the defining aspect of what it means to be human, it is lifted above the rest of our person in various ways. This erroneous thinking emerges regarding the unborn when it is wrongly said that a baby does not have total human worth unless their brain or body functions at a certain level otherwise they are not a fully valued person.

The third error regarding imago Dei occurs when we define our humanity in terms of things we do. Called the functional view, it emphasizes a human function, usually the exercise of dominion over creation.[60] The problem with this view is that those who are not able to function as most people do would logically be considered somehow less human than the rest of us. The unborn, sick, comatose, elderly, and infirm are as much image bearers of God as those who can do certain things which is why advocates of abortion, infanticide, and forced sterilizations believe they are justified in ending these lives.

In sum, Christians believe five things regarding the idea of imago Dei. (1) Human beings alone are God's image bearers. (2) As God's image bearers, human beings are under God and over lower creation, and great error arises when they are pulled up toward God or pushed down toward animals. (3) Human beings are the image of God, and this fact is not reduced to any aspect of their person or performance. (4) As God's image bearers, human beings have particular dignity, value, and worth. (5) As God's image bearers, humans were made to mirror God as an act of worship, which is only possible as we turn toward God.

In the first chapter we established that an unborn child is a living human being according to science. In this chapter we have established that human beings uniquely bear the image of God and that human life is, therefore, uniquely sacred.

bones in the **womb** of a woman and knit me together with bon
you do not know the work of God sinews.
verything. You have granted me life and steadf
and your care has preserved my
it was, declares the Lord God. "And yo
ldren are a heritage from th your sons and your daughters, whom y
of the womb a reward. borne to me, and these you sacrificed t
s in the hand of a warrior to be devoured. Were your whorings s
hildren of one's youth. a matter ²¹ that you **slaughtered my c**
he man and delivered them up as an offering
s his quiver with them! to them? will be exalted."

"Who is the greatest in the ki **Let the Children Come to Me**
n?" ²And calling to him a child ¹⁵ Now they were bringing eve
e midst of them ³and said, "Tr him that he might touch them. A
unless you turn and become disciples saw it, they rebuked them
will never enter the kingdom called them to him, saying, "Let
oever humbles himself like come to me, and do not hinder
reatest in the kingdom of hea such belongs the kingdom of God.
come to me? "For behold, when to you, whoever does not receive
f your greeting came to my ears, God like a child shall not enter
my **womb leaped for joy**. ⁴⁵ And ich Ruler
of all and servant of all." ³⁶And he son of Hinnom, to burn
and put him in the midst of them, daughters in the fire, whi
him in his arms, he said to them, mand, nor did it come into
receives one such child in my name efore, behold, the days are c
and whoever receives me, receives and obtains favor from
him who sent me." ut he who fails to find me
all who hate me love de

lav of Wisdom
for I am **fearfully and wonder** father's desires. He was a murde
made.¹ beginning, and does not stand
ust not drink wine or stror
e filled with the Holy Spir Before I formed you in the womb I
ther's womb. ¹⁶And he v you,
hildren of Israel to the L and before you were born I consecr
you;

27 SCRIPTURES ABOUT THE UNBORN

Romans 10:17 (NKJV) – ...faith comes by...hearing by the word of God.

The first few times I read the Bible, I did not agree with it. This is the same experience of everyone I have ever spoken to. The Bible is a book that conflicts, corrects, and challenges what we believe. In some ways, it is like an anvil on which everything gets hammered out, but it does not change shape no matter how many blows it is dealt.

Whether or not you believe that the Bible is God's Word to us, it is integrous to at least consider what it says. When we are dealing with important matters, as a general rule, it is best to hear both sides before rendering a verdict like any judge presiding over a court. In this chapter, we will briefly examine the primary Scriptures about the unborn going in the order they appear in most English Bibles.

1. God is pro-life. God's intent was that human beings would marry, have generations of children, and fill the entire planet with human life.
   Genesis 1:28 (ESV) – God blessed them. And God said to them, "Be fruitful and multiply and fill the earth and subdue it, and have dominion..."

2. God is anti-death. Although God gave people the freedom to eat animals just a few verses prior (Genesis 9:3), He declares that human life is uniquely sacred and to wrongly terminate human life is a capital offense.
Genesis 9:6 (ESV) "Whoever sheds the blood of man, by man shall his blood be shed, for God made man in his own image."
3. God sees the unborn as children. Here, twin brothers wresting in the womb are reported. Importantly, "The word for 'children' in this passage is the normal Old Testament word translated 'sons' (Gen. 5:4, 7, 10; Prov. 7:7)."[61] This Hebrew word appears over 4,900 times in the Old Testament and is translated "son", "sons" or "children".
Genesis 25:22 (ESV) – The children struggled together within her, and she said, "If it is thus, why is this happening to me?" So she went to inquire of the Lord.
4. God's people are pro-life and practice civil disobedience. The godless Egyptian government commanded infanticide of the Hebrew boys, but godly pro-life women practiced civil disobedience and are honored by God for doing so.[a]
Exodus 1:16–17 (ESV) – "When you serve as midwife to the Hebrew women and see them on the birthstool, if it is a son, you shall kill him, but if it is a daughter, she shall live. But the midwives feared God and did not do as the king of Egypt commanded them, but let the male children live."
5. Murder is a sin and a crime. In the list of the 10 Commandments, God is clear that murder is both a sin against Him and a legal crime in the 6th Commandment. Some people wrongly translate the Hebrew word found here as "kill", which would relate to the taking of any human life. However, the original Hebrew word is best translated "murder" which is the taking of an innocent human life, such as an unborn child. One Bible dictionary

---

[a] Hebrews 11:23

says, "This prohibition of murder (חָצַר, ratsach) upholds the idea that human life holds value because God created humans in His image.[a] While the translation 'kill' is not technically improper, the term is better translated as 'murder', since capital punishment is mandated in both the Noahic covenant, Exodus,[b] and Deuteronomy.[c] The relation between humans and the image of God essentially equates murder with the killing of a god."[62]
Exodus 20:13 (ESV) – "You shall not murder."

6. A preborn child has legal rights. The first five books of the Old Testament are called the books of the Law because they provide the legal framework for God's Old Covenant people. In this law, an unborn child is clearly seen as a full human being with full legal rights and when their life is taken, murder has been committed and capital punishment is mandated.
Exodus 21:22-25 (ESV) – "When men strive together and hit a pregnant woman, so that her children come out, but there is no harm, the one who hit her shall surely be fined, as the woman's husband shall impose on him, and he shall pay as the judges determine. But if there is harm, then you shall pay life for life, eye for eye, tooth for tooth, hand for hand, foot for foot, burn for burn, wound for wound, stripe for stripe."

7. It is demonic to kill your child. In the days of the Old Testament, God's people were surrounded by nations that sacrificed their own children to demon gods, which was abhorrent to God. Therefore, they were forbidden from terminating the life of their child.
Leviticus 18:21 (ESV) – You shall not give any of your children to offer them to Molech, and so profane the name of your God: I am the LORD.

8. Physicians should not tear apart what the Great Physician has

---

[a]Gen 9:6 [b]e.g., Exod. 19:13; 21:14; 32:27 [c]e.g., Deut. 13:10; 17:5; 19:12; 22:21

knit together. In our church I was speaking to a medical doctor who explained that he entered medical school as an atheist and exited as a Christian. He explained that studying the incredible intricacy of human life beginning in the womb brought him to believe that there is a loving and living God who created us. Today, he is a pro-life doctor who says that physicians should not tear apart in the womb what the Great Physician has knit together in the womb.

Job 10:11–12 (ESV) – You clothed me with skin and flesh, and knit me together with bones and sinews. You have granted me life and steadfast love, and your care has preserved my spirit.

9. God works in the womb. Human life comes from God who makes us in our mother's womb. The Bible is repeatedly clear on this point without equivocation.

    Job 31:15 (ESV) – Did not he who made me in the womb make him? And did not one fashion us in the womb?

10. A preborn child is known by God. In this reflection back on the wonder of life, we are told that babies are dependent upon their God from their mother's womb, through their birth, and into their adult life.

    Psalm 71:6 (ESV) – Upon you I have leaned from before my birth; you are he who took me from my mother's womb. My praise is continually of you.

11. Children are a blessing. Life is a blessing, and having new life added through birth is a blessing from God, who is the Living God and source of life. Life is so cherished by God's people that barrenness brings deep grief and is common throughout the patriarchs including Sarai,[a] Rebekah,[b] and Rachel[c] though God eventually answered each of their prayers and enabled them to conceive, which brought them joy. In the New Testament, Elizabeth refers to her many years of barrenness before birthing

---

[a]Genesis 11:30, 16:1-2 [b]Genesis 25:21 [c]Genesis 29:31

John the Baptizer as "disgrace", "reproach", "humiliation" or "shame" in various English translations of Luke 1:25. The thought of a Hebrew woman ending the life of her child was simply inconceivable because the baby was God's blessing. A theological journal says, "For both sexes, the only known form of immortality was through producing offspring. Procreation raised the social status of both parents, especially of the mother. The barren woman was regarded with reproach (Gen 30:23; I Sam 1:6; Tobit 3:7–9; and Luke 1:25). There being no old-age pensions or homes for the aged, a large number of children was insurance against destitution after a person became too ill or too old to work. Given such a mentality and social organization, no person in the cultural milieu of the Old Testament would ever seek an abortion."[63]

Psalm 127:3–5 (ESV) – Behold, children are a heritage from the Lord, the fruit of the womb a reward. Like arrows in the hand of a warrior are the children of one's youth. Blessed is the man who fills his quiver with them!

12. God knows us from the womb. Long before ultrasound allowed us to peer into the mystery of life in the womb, God who sees and knows all reports that He knew us and knit us from our mother's womb with a body and soul made wonderfully by Him.
Psalm 139:13-14 (ESV) – For you formed my inward parts; you knitted me together in my mother's womb. I praise you, for I am fearfully and wonderfully made. Wonderful are your works; my soul knows it very well.

13. To hate life is to hate the Living God. God is the Father of life, and Satan is the father of murder Jesus' says.[a] All who love God love life, and all those who hate God love death.
Proverbs 8:36 – "…all who hate me love death."

14. A preborn child has a soul. There is admittedly a debate as to

---

[a] John 8:44

when a physical body receives a spiritual soul. Since the soul is unseen, it is not surprising that the answer to this question is a mystery. This is precisely what this section of Scripture says, as God alone knows, but one thing is sure – we are told that a baby in the womb has a soul in their body.

Ecclesiastes 11:5 (ESV) – As you do not know the way the spirit comes to the bones in the womb of a woman with child, so you do not know the work of God who makes everything.

15. God calls us from the womb. From the womb, God sees us as a person who is known by Him, set aside for a destiny in our life, and expected to be born to fulfill His will for our lives. God is clear that He knows us long before we know Him, and His relationship with us starts in our mother's womb.

    Jeremiah 1:5 (ESV) – "Before I formed you in the womb I knew you, and before you were born I consecrated you; I appointed you a prophet to the nations."

16. Killing children is not from the mind of God. Theologians are fond to speak of God's omniscience, which means that God alone is all-knowing. Here, God tells His people that taking the innocent lives of their own children is not an idea that they received from Him as it is literally a godless thing to even think let alone do.

    Jeremiah 7:31–32 (ESV) – ...they have built the high places of Topheth, which is in the Valley of the Son of Hinnom, to burn their sons and their daughters in the fire, which I did not command, nor did it come into my mind.

17. When sex is a demonic religion, children are the sacrifice. What God creates Satan counterfeits. In Christianity, Jesus Christ the Son of God comes to earth to die for our sins. In demonic counterfeit religions that worship sex, the worshippers sacrifice their own sons and daughters to demons.

    Ezekiel 16:20–21 (ESV) – ...you took your sons and your

daughters, whom you had borne to me, and these you sacrificed to them to be devoured. Were your whorings so small a matter that you slaughtered my children and delivered them up as an offering by fire to them?

18. Evil governments take the life of children. In the days when Jesus was born, the godless government ruled by a demonic dictator wanted to kill Jesus and so he sent out a decree to terminate the lives of Hebrew baby boys. God's people have always been pro-life, and demonic governments have always been pro-death, especially of God's people. The governments change from age to age, but the demons do not and today these same demons are pushing the same agenda through new governments.
    Matthew 2:16 (ESV) – …Herod…became furious, and he sent and killed all the male children in Bethlehem and in all that region…
19. Jesus so loves children that He associates with their suffering. Throughout His ministry, children gathered around Jesus because He loved them, blessed them, and was safe for them. Of course, Jesus can and does save us from any and every sin, but for those who reject Jesus and harm children there is judgment and justice from Jesus.
    Matthew 18:5–6 (ESV) – "Whoever receives one such child in my name receives me, but whoever causes one of these little ones who believe in me to sin, it would be better for him to have a great millstone fastened around his neck and to be drowned in the depth of the sea."
20. What you really think about Jesus is revealed in how you treat children. The way we think about Jesus is reflected in how we treat children, according to His own words. Jesus so identifies with children that to reject them is to reject Him. Any Christian who is not pro-life is not pro-Jesus.

Mark 9:36–37 (ESV) – And he took a child and put him in the midst of them, and taking him in his arms, he said to them, "Whoever receives one such child in my name receives me, and whoever receives me, receives not me but him who sent me."

21. Children are a blessing to be blessed. Children are a blessing that God gives us to bless. The opposite of blessing is cursing. To harm or kill a child in the womb is to curse the blessing that God has given us and to curse God.

    Mark 10:16 (ESV) – And he [Jesus] took them [children] in his arms and blessed them, laying his hands on them.

22. Children can be born again before they are born. John the Baptizer had a name, calling, destiny, and the Holy Spirit from His mother's womb. This is an incredibly clear and undeniable proof that life begins in the womb.

    Luke 1:15 (ESV) – …he [John the Baptizer] will be filled with the Holy Spirit, even from his mother's womb.

23. Jesus Christ is Mary's son from her womb. Mary was chosen to be the earthly mother of Jesus Christ because she was "favored" by God to have a "son" named Jesus who would be a person from the time she was set to "conceive" in her "womb". Mary accepted this ministry mission of motherhood as a sacred and blessed calling from God to be a mom.

    Luke 1:26-38 (ESV) – …the angel Gabriel was sent from God to a city of Galilee named Nazareth, to a virgin…[whose] name was Mary. And he came to her and said, "Greetings, O favored one, the Lord is with you!" But she was greatly troubled at the saying, and tried to discern what sort of greeting this might be. And the angel said to her, "Do not be afraid, Mary, for you have found favor with God. And behold, you will conceive in your womb and bear a son, and you shall call his name Jesus. He will be great and will be called the Son of the Most High. And the Lord God will give to him the throne of his father

David, and he will reign over the house of Jacob forever, and of his kingdom there will be no end." And Mary said to the angel, "How will this be, since I am a virgin?" And the angel answered her, "The Holy Spirit will come upon you, and the power of the Most High will overshadow you; therefore the child to be born will be called holy—the Son of God" …And Mary said, "Behold, I am the servant of the Lord; let it be to me according to your word." And the angel departed from her.

24. John the Baptizer is Elizabeth's son from her womb. Elizabeth is overjoyed that, after a lifetime of barrenness, she is given the blessing of becoming the mother of John the Baptizer. Even though John is not yet born, he has been "conceived" and God declares her unborn child her "son" through the angel Gabriel.
Luke 1:36-37 (ESV) – [the angel Gabriel said to Mary], "And behold, your relative Elizabeth in her old age has also conceived a son, and this is the sixth month with her who was called barren. For nothing will be impossible with God."

25. Children can worship from the womb. When Mary and Elizabeth came together, the boys in their bellies were Jesus Christ and John the Baptizer. When John came near the presence of Jesus Christ even from his mom's tummy he recognized and responded to the presence of God and worshipped. This may indicate that sometimes when a baby is active in their mother's womb, they may be worshipping God as well.
Luke 1:41,44 (ESV) – …when Elizabeth heard the greeting of Mary, the baby leaped in her womb…the baby in my [Elizabeth] womb leaped for joy.

26. God came to the earth through Mary's womb. When Jesus Christ entered human history, He could have shown up at any age. Jesus chose to come as an unborn baby, to begin his life on earth in Mary's womb, and to be birthed as we all are. Nothing could more honor the sacred gift of life from the womb than the

coming of Jesus Christ in this very way.
Luke 2:12,16 (ESV) – ...you will find a baby wrapped in swaddling cloths and lying in a manger...they went with haste and found Mary and Joseph, and the baby lying in a manger.

27. Children in and out of the womb are the same to God. The medical doctor, Luke, writes more of the New Testament than anyone. The Holy Spirit, who knows life in the womb, says the following through Dr. Luke who uses the same Greek word in every verse below:
Luke 1:41 (ESV) – ...when Elizabeth heard the greeting of Mary, the baby [John the Baptizer] leaped in her womb.
Luke 1:44 (ESV) – ...the baby [John the Baptizer] in my [Elizabeth's] womb leaped for joy.
Luke 2:12 (ESV) – ...you will find a baby [Jesus] wrapped in swaddling cloths and lying in a manger.
Luke 2:16 (ESV) – ...they went with haste and found Mary and Joseph, and the baby [Jesus] lying in a manger.
Luke 18:15 (ESV) – Now they were bringing even infants to him [Jesus] that he might touch them.
Acts 7:9 (ESV) – He [Pharoah] dealt shrewdly with our race and forced our fathers to expose their infants, so that they would not be kept alive.

    Scripture uses the same word (*brephos*) for Elizabeth's unborn child (John the Baptizer), newborn baby Jesus, and also for the children brought to Jesus, along with kids killed in the Old Testament. Simply, in the divinely inspired pages of Scripture, God reveals to us that a child in the womb and a child singing and dancing around Jesus in worship are equally human beings, who bear the image of God. Not to extend legal protections to preborn children because of age, size, or phase of development is a grievous discrimination and injustice akin to racism, sexism, and ageism. God values all human life, including the unborn, as we will learn next as we study the earthly life of our God and Savior Jesus Christ from His mother's womb with an emphasis on the writings of the early church historian and medical doctor, Luke.

GOD BECAME A ZYGOTE

Matthew 1:25 (ESV) – "Behold, the virgin shall conceive and bear a son, and they shall call his name Immanuel (which means, God with us)."

Ancient Christian creeds tell us that God became a man. Technically, that is true. However, before Jesus Christ became a man, He became a very little man.

We tend to think of Jesus as a grown man hiking over rough terrain, sleeping outside in the elements, fighting demons, curing the sick, preaching the gospel, and fighting the religious neatnicks. Jesus did all of this, and more. However, before he was walking around as a grown man, he was being carried around as a zygote in the womb of His mother Mary.

Theologian J. I. Packer has described the incarnation as the "supreme mystery" associated with the gospel.[64] He goes on to explain that the incarnation is more of a miracle than the resurrection because in it somehow a holy God and sinful humanity are joined, yet without the presence of sin: "Nothing in fiction is so fantastic as is this truth of the incarnation."[65]

Stop to consider, for a moment, that the God who made everything Himself became an unborn baby, vulnerable and dependent upon His loving Mother. Theologians like to say that God became a man to identify with our humanity, which is true. However,

God became a baby to identify with their humanity as well. No one has more insight to the womb, or sympathy for those in the womb, than our God and Savior, Jesus Christ. He knows exactly what it is like to be an unborn baby that is born into the world who then grows into adulthood.

Consider for a moment the growing life of a child in their mother's womb and imagine Jesus Christ, our Creator, entering creation to undergo this process. A summary of human development says, "Human beings develop at an astonishingly rapid pace. Giving a quick recitation of the child's development will weaken the 'not a person yet' mentality…The cardiovascular system is the first major system to function. At about 22 days after conception the child's heart begins to circulate his own blood, unique from that of his mother's, and his heartbeat can be detected on ultrasound… At just six weeks, the child's eyes and eyelids, nose, mouth, and tongue have formed….Electrical brain activity can be detected at six or seven weeks, and by the end of the eighth week, the child, now known scientifically as a 'fetus,' has developed all of his organs and bodily structures…By ten weeks after conception the child can make bodily movements. From as early as 12 weeks—and certainly by 20 weeks—an unborn child can feel pain…The obstetric ultrasound done typically at 20 weeks gestation provides not only pictures but a real-time video of the active life of the child in the womb: clasping his hands, sucking his thumb, yawning, stretching, getting the hiccups, covering his ears to a loud sound nearby… —even smiling."[66]

MARY CHOSE CHRIST OVER THE CLINIC

For Christians, the abortion debate hits close to home. Mary was probably a teenager, poor, possibly uneducated, living in a small rural town. She was not wanting or planning to have a child, which explains why she remained a virgin until after she was married. Mary got pregnant out of wedlock by a miracle of God the Holy Spirit in a highly religious ancient cultural context. She is facing a life as a poor, likely uneducated, very young mother with a ruined reputation in a religious small town.

If she walked into a clinic today, we know what she would be encouraged to do. But Mary gave birth to God. Jesus came into the world through the womb of a woman who fits the stereotype of someone who "should" get an abortion. Thankfully, Mary courageously brought Jesus into the world so that He could save the world from death.

Mary is a relative of Elizabeth, but when Luke picks up the narrative, Mary does not yet know that her elderly cousin is pregnant. Mary is merely a young woman living a quiet life in Nazareth. We will briefly summarize the story of Mary's pregnancy from Luke 1-2.

Neither the Old Testament nor other significant historical texts mention Nazareth. It's a nowhere town where nothing important happens.

After his visit with Zechariah within the sacred walls of the temple in Jerusalem, where does God send the angel Gabriel next? Nazareth, to meet with Mary.

Mary is betrothed to Joseph, meaning they have pledged to marry each other in an arrangement far more serious and binding than what we understand as engagement today. In a small rural town where kids grew up together and most everyone operated like one big extended family, to publicly declare engagement was something only done if the bride and groom to-be were fully committed to walking down the aisle.

Most theologians believe Mary is somewhere between 12 and 14 years old at the time when Gabriel pays her a visit. Let that sink in.

Everything is riding on a teenage girl. Now that's faith.

Gabriel tells Mary the amazing news: your son will be named Jesus, which means God saves from sins. Her son will be God's Son and her Savior.

Mary's response to God's plan is legendary: "Behold, I am the servant of the Lord; let it be to me according to your word".[a] She is a humble young woman with simple but sincere faith. Mary believes God. Her son will one day emulate this simple, courageous resolve. In the Garden of Gethsemane, as Jesus atones for the sins of the world through the shedding of His blood, He says, "Your will be done".[b] There are moments in His life when Jesus echoes His godly mother.

Unmarried. Poor. Young. Pregnant with God. Mary has a lot to worry about. Rather than worrying, Mary starts worshipping. Her beautiful, spontaneous, anointed, song begins with the words, "My soul magnifies the Lord."[c] Her spirit and the Holy Spirit intersect to worship.

Culturally, we may not completely appreciate what Mary and Joseph are willing to sacrifice. Mary risks losing her fiancé. She does lose her reputation. (Small town religious gossip can be brutal.) Joseph's boy Jesus is called illegitimate, his wife is called unfaithful, and he is called a fool for the rest of his life. He doesn't have to accept this fate and can cancel the wedding. He is seemingly a strong and steady kind of guy who does a lot more than he says. We know he has numerous angelic visits and every time he is told to do something, he obeys the Lord no matter what the cost.

Since Jesus will not be his biological son, Joseph stands as a bit of a hero for foster parents, adoption, and blended families. He appears to be a quiet, humble, godly man whose most significant ministry will turn out to be working an honest job, loving his wife, obeying God, and raising godly kids who change the world. Thanks to

[a]*Luke 1:38* [b]*Matt. 26:42* [c]*Luke 1:46*

Joseph's humble obedience, Jesus will have a devoted dad.

The Spirit is so active in the life of this family that even their pastor prophesies at Jesus' baby dedication at the temple. Mary and Joseph travel about 140 miles from Nazareth to Jerusalem to dedicate Jesus in the temple. This takes them roughly one week, so we know that this very devout family does "according to what is said in the Law of the Lord".[a]

Once in Jerusalem, Joseph and Mary meet an old covenant pastor named Simeon who loves God. Luke 2:26–27 says, "It had been revealed to him by the Holy Spirit that he would not see death before he had seen the Lord's Christ. And he came in the Spirit into the temple…" Simeon then praises God for Jesus and prophesies salvation and suffering for the Savior.

Joseph and Mary encounter another Holy Spirit-inspired prophecy during their trip. Anna, a prophetess, praises God for the opportunity to witness "the redemption of Jerusalem".[b] After these powerful encounters with the Spirit of God, Joseph, Mary, and Jesus complete their ceremonies and start home again for Nazareth.

Not only were Jesus' "aunt" Elizabeth, "uncle", mom, dad, baby-dedicating pastor, and prophetess Spirit-filled, so was Jesus' cousin.

JESUS' COUSIN JOHN WAS SPIRIT-FILLED FROM THE WOMB

Excited to see her relative Elizabeth and celebrate their pregnancies, Mary walks about a hundred miles, maybe by herself, likely in the hot sun, alone.

As we pick up the story, we see Mary's immediate obedience to God's word in Luke 1:39–40, "In those days Mary arose and went with haste into the hill country, to a town in Judah, and she entered the house of Zechariah and greeted Elizabeth."

[a]Luke 2:24 [b]Luke 2:38

In the culture of the New Testament, society often marginalized women, particularly those who were young, poor, and single, and those who were elderly, poor, and childless. This was especially true if they lived away from major urban centers and lacked connections to influential families. Mary and Elizabeth fit all those criteria. They were among the least likely to be chosen for something significant.

About 25 percent of our Bible was prophetic (predicting future events) when written. Sometimes prophecy is a personal message; God wants someone to know something, so He sends a messenger to deliver a word to that individual. This is the kind of prophecy we see from Elizabeth. Luke 1:41–42 tells us, "Elizabeth was filled with the Holy Spirit, and she exclaimed with a loud cry, 'Blessed are you among women, and blessed is the fruit of your womb!'"

Elizabeth continues to honor Mary, which is unusual since it would be customary for the younger to honor the older. Not only does she honor Mary, but Elizabeth also honors Mary's baby.

"And why is this granted to me that the mother of my Lord should come to me?" asks Elizabeth.[a] She hasn't seen Jesus walk on water, raise the dead, heal people, die on a cross, or resurrect from death—she hasn't even seen Him be born—but Elizabeth is astounded to come near Jesus, and she worships Him and claims Him as her Lord. Being in the presence of the pre-born Lord was all she needed to be inspired to worship Him. In fact, Elizabeth is the first person in the New Testament to worship Jesus Christ!

In the next moment, the two women draw near one another, and with them the two sons who represent the old covenant and the new covenant; the promises and the fulfillment; the prophet and the Lord. Their bellies come together—and Elizabeth's unborn son John worships along with his mother! Luke 1:41 reports, "the baby leaped in her womb. And Elizabeth was filled with the Holy Spirit."

This is incredible.

---

[a]Luke 1:43

John is known by God, filled with the Spirit, and named with a calling of destiny on his life—all before he's ever seen the sunshine, felt the wind, or sipped fresh air into his lungs. He is filled with the Holy Spirit, and we get our first glimpse of John as an in-utero worship leader, dancing and celebrating in the womb. I can't think of a stronger portrait of personhood in the womb than that.

Luke, a medical doctor, writes under the inspiration of God the Holy Spirit. What does it mean when he says of Elizabeth that, "the baby leaped in her womb"?

A baby in a womb is known by God as John was, named by God as John was, and can be filled with God the Holy Spirit as John was.[a] How wonderful is it that God cares about unborn children? How encouraging is it that, even when children are miscarried or aborted, we see the possibility that God can know them, love them, name them, and fill them with the Spirit, even from the womb as He did John?

If we took a poll to name the most significant person history has ever known, it's highly unlikely that John the Baptizer would even crack the top ten or top thousand. Jesus is in a category of His own: God incarnate. Regarding John's greatness, we read in Luke 1:15, that John "will be great before the Lord." Jesus makes it even clearer saying, "I tell you, among those born of women none is greater than John".[b]

What was so great about this bug-eating, honey-chugging, gospel-preaching, sinner-baptizing, Jedi robe-wearing eccentric? John lived his entire life by the Spirit's power. Before John's birth, the angel Gabriel said, "He will be filled with the Holy Spirit, even from his mother's womb".[c] The Bible also says, "The hand of the Lord was with him".[d] That's another way of saying that the Holy Spirit was present with him, in him, and through him for his entire life. John became the greatest man who ever lived, except for Jesus, by the

[a]*Luke 1:15* [b]*Luke 7:28* [c]*Luke 1:15* [d]*Luke 1:66*

power of the Holy Spirit.

John was a bit of a wild man who grew up in the wilderness and was not owned by the religious establishment. He was young, charismatic, strong, eccentric, and fearless. Crowds flocked to him like a breakout rock star or revolutionary young politician.

John was not all about John. John was all about Jesus. "After me comes he who is mightier than I," John said, "the strap of whose sandals I am not worthy to stoop down and untie".[a] In that day, a student would do anything and everything for their teacher with one exception – remove their sandals, a job reserved for the lowest-ranking slave. Even with his stock at an all-time high and his first tour just starting and the t-shirts rolling off the press, John said he was unworthy to do the work of a slave for Jesus Christ. When his fame was hotter than ever and he could have cashed it all in for a huge ministry, he set it all aside, sent all his disciples to follow Jesus, and said, "He must increase, but I must decrease".[b]

John's public ministry lasted roughly six months—shorter than an academic freshman year at a Bible college. He preached a lot of sermons, baptized perhaps thousands of people, handed his ministry to Jesus, and got martyred—all by the age of about 30.

Many, if not most, of Jesus' early followers were originally part of John's ministry. John accepted his role as the opening band and exited the stage once the crowd was warmed up, Jesus was ready to take the stage and the Church was ready to be released on the earth by the Spirit following His resurrection in defeat of sin and death.

The greatest movement of any sort or kind in the history of the world is the Christian faith. Jesus Christ looms so largely over history that we measure historical time in the context of His life. BC refers to the time "before Christ," and AD (anno Domini) means "in the year of the Lord". Our biggest holidays are dedicated to Him as we celebrate His birth every Christmas and resurrection every Easter.

[a]Mark 1:7 [b]John 3:30

Nations, causes, and leaders have come and gone. But for more than 2,000 years, the Church of Jesus Christ has spread from one nation to the nations, from the language of Hebrew to thousands of languages, and from one generation to generation after generation. Christianity ranks as the most popular religion and largest and longest-standing movement of any kind in the history of the planet with more than two billion people today claiming to be followers of Jesus Christ.

Approaching the new millennium, *Newsweek* ran a cover story that said, "By any secular standard, Jesus is also the dominant figure of Western culture. Like the millennium itself, much of what we now think of as Western ideas, inventions and values finds its source or inspiration in the religion that worships God in his name. Art and science, the self and society, politics and economics, marriage and the family, right and wrong, body and soul—all have been touched and often radically transformed by the Christian influence."[67]

Surveying the record of human life on the planet, perhaps historian Kenneth Scott Latourette has said it best, "Jesus is the most influential life ever lived on this planet."[68]

Human history would be completely different if it were not for John the Baptizer paving the way for the coming of Jesus Christ. Their lives began with the divine announcement that they would be sons with names and destinies from their mother's wombs. Jesus' mother Mary would today be a candidate for an abortion because of her poverty, singleness, social status, and unplanned pregnancy. John's mother Elizabeth would today be a candidate for an abortion because she was elderly and had been barren her entire life, making this an unplanned, high-risk pregnancy. Thankfully, Jesus' mother Mary was pro-life, as God's people have always been which we will study next.

24% OF ALL WOMEN HAVE ABORTIONS BY AGE 45

17% OF ABORTING WOMEN CLAIMED TO BE MAIN LINE PROTESTANT

13% OF ABORTING WOMEN CLAIMED TO BE EVANGELICAL PROTESTANT

24% OF ABORTING WOMEN CLAIMED TO BE CATHOLIC

38% OF ABORTING WOMEN CLAIMED NO RELIGIOUS AFFILIATION

8% OF ABORTING WOMEN CLAIMED SOME OTHER AFFILIATION

guttmacher.org

7

CHRISTIANS HAVE ALWAYS BEEN PRO-LIFE

John 10:10 (ESV) – The thief comes only to steal and kill and destroy. I came that they may have life and have it abundantly.

Throughout the Roman Empire, it was common for children to be severely beaten and even tossed out into the garbage or dung heap to either die or be taken by someone and used for their purposes (i.e. a slave, prostitute, gladiator, etc.). Infant mortality was so high that only half of children lived to their fifth birthday, and less than 40% lived until their 20th birthday. Consequently, a family would need to birth five children to have two, and usually waited between eight and nine days after the birth to name the child to see if they lived through the first week. Poorer families often had children to help earn income and care for them when they grew old. Infanticide was common, particularly with disabled children and girls, and included abandonment in the desert, being thrown in a river tied to a rock, and even suffocation by the hand of their parent. Contraception and abortion of varying kinds were also common in the ancient world.

Since the earliest days of the Church of Jesus Christ, Christians also took strides toward social equality—especially when it came to unwanted children. Children in the time of Jesus often lacked legal protection or parental affection. Sacrificing and abandoning children was common. Discarded children often died from exposure or were taken as slaves, prostitutes, or gladiators. This was especially true for children from the bottom rungs of society. But that's just where Jesus came from. He was the King of the Universe come as a baby to a poor rural family. In a society that dismissed and abused children regularly, Jesus loved kids and kids loved Him. They flocked to Jesus, and He welcomed, embraced, and prayed over them, as we learn from some of the fondest Bible stories ever. Because of His example, Christians began to treat children differently, including adopting discarded children. That work still continues with orphanages, foster care, and adoptions around the world developed and operated by Christians who have God's heart for the value of all children from all backgrounds.

GOD'S PEOPLE HAVE ALWAYS BEEN PRO-LIFE

Christians have always followed the teaching of the Old Testament Jews, that abortion of a pre-born child and exposure of a born child are both murderous sins. The Epistle of Barnabas, a Christian writing from the days of the early Church says, "Thou shalt not procure abortion, thou shalt not commit infanticide."[69]

According to the *Didache*, which was a ministry manual for leaders in the early church, abortion was murder. We read, "According to Did 5:2, among those who are on the 'Way of Death' are 'infanticides' and 'those destroying the image of God' [cf. Epistle of Barnabas 20:2] Apparently, then, the fetus was viewed as being a neighbor with the same rights—including the right to life—that the neighbor would have."[70] It was common for the early church fathers to preach and teach against abortion. We read, "John Chrysostom in the East and Jerome in the West both condemned it."[71] Other examples include:

The *Didache*, one of the most prominent extrabiblical early church documents, explicitly forbids abortion: "Do not abort a fetus or kill a child that is born".[72]

Basil declared that a woman who had induced an abortion should be tried for murder.[73]

Augustine extensively spoke against abortion, particularly as he wrestled with theological issues such as the existence of the soul.[74]

In the first few hundred years of Christianity, the discussion of abortion revolved around when the unborn fetus actually became human. Although not all Christian writers were explicitly anti-abortion,[75] by the Middle Ages, most Christians condemned the practice[76] [77].

In the earliest days of the Christian Church, there were debates on most every issue and, over time the majority view as led by the Holy Spirit guided God's people into unified truth. This was the case for the doctrine of the Trinity, deity and humanity of Christ, and abhorrence of abortion among innumerable other issues. In every season of Church history, there have always been a few outliers, apostates, and heretics as there are in our own day. But, make no mistake, God's people from the Old Testament to the present guided by the Scriptures and the Spirit have always been pro-life. Just like a variety of church councils produced decrees about various doctrinal issues, the Council of Elvira included a forbidding of abortion among its 81 decrees (306 AD). Additionally, the Church Council of Ancyra in 314 A.D. also forbid abortion and those who encouraged others to have an abortion.

A few more examples will help stress this important truth. History reports that Christian leaders, "*Barnabas, *Athenagoras, *Clement of Alexandria, *Tertullian, Sts *Ambrose, *Chrysostom, *Jerome, and *Augustine were united in their condemnation of infanticide and abortion, in contrast to their pagan contemporaries."[78]

In the second century, one of the great defenders, Athenagros, was brought before the emperor to defend Christianity against three false accusations. He said, "What reason would we have to commit murder when we say that women who induce abortions are murderers, and will have to give account of it to God? For the same person would not regard the fetus in the womb as a living thing and therefore an object of God's care [and then kill it]...But we are altogether consistent in our conduct. We obey reason and do not override it..."[79]

Tertullian, also in the second century, is one of the most famous and cited early church fathers. He writes, "In our case, murder being once for all forbidden, we may not destroy even the fetus in the womb, while as yet the human being derives blood from other parts of the body for its sustenance. To hinder a birth is merely a speedier man-killing; nor does it matter whether you take away a life that is born or destroy one that is coming to the birth. That is a man which is going to be one; you have the fruit already in the seed."[80]

Marcus Minucius Felix, the third-century defender of Christianity, wrote to rebut the fake news report that Christians take the lives of children. He spoke against the horror that, "there are women who swallow drugs to stifle in their own womb the beginnings of a man to be-committing infanticide before they give birth to the infant."[81]

In the fifth century, Augustine, who is one of the most significant Christian thinkers in Church history, spoke out clearly against abortion. His statements include, "Sometimes, indeed, this lustful cruelty, or, if you please, cruel lust, resorts to such extravagant methods as to use poisonous drugs to secure barrenness; or else, if unsuccessful in this, to destroy the conceived seed by some means previous to birth, preferring that its offspring should rather perish than receive vitality; or if it was advancing to life within the womb, should be slain before it was born."[82]

One of the greatest minds in the history of Christian theology is John Calvin who said, "Wherefore this, in my opinion, is the meaning of the law, that it would be a crime punishable with death, not only when the mother died from the effects of the abortion, but also if the infant should be killed; whether it should die from the wound abortively, or soon after its birth.' Since this punishment is the same as that for killing a full-grown man (Gen. 9:6; Exod. 21:12; Lev. 24:17), it demonstrates that God considers the child in the womb as real and as valuable a person as an adult."[83]

ABORTION IS ANCIENT AND, IN MANY PLACES, COMMON

The consistent opposition of God's people to abortion throughout the ages is intriguing considering the frequent strong cultural support of abortion. One Bible dictionary says, "Abortion has been practiced for millennia; through most of history, it was induced by herbal chemistry. Both contraceptives and abortion-inducing agents were used by a variety of cultures. An inscription from ancient Sumer lists what is likely a recipe for inducing abortion, and Egyptian papyri dating as far back as 1500 bc make references to chemicals being used to induce abortion.[84] The earliest medical writing from Egypt, dated around 1850 bc, contains recipes for preventing conception.[85] Chemically induced abortions appear to have been attempted in ancient Sumer, Assyria, Egypt, Greece, and Rome. Euripides indicates that women practiced abortion at the time of the Trojan Wars.[86] Pliny the Elder (ad 23–79) wrote about various herbs that could induce an abortion and recorded superstitions about inducing abortion, such as having a woman step over a crow's egg.[87] Orally administered and externally applied drugs, including chemicals and herbal substances, were used to attempt to induce abortion, but physical means were also known to be used. A surgical procedure to remove a fetus may have existed as far back as the first century AD."[88] [89]

Because God created us with a conscience, there have been leaders who have spoken out against abortion throughout history. Even people without the Scriptures and the Spirit have historically defended the pro-life position. For example, the code of Hammurabi from roughly 1728 B.C. contained prohibitions against abortions. According to the National Library of Medicine, in his oaths to physicians, Hippocrates included, "I will give no deadly medicine to anyone if asked, nor suggest any such counsel; and in like manner I will not give to a woman a pessary to produce abortion."[90] In addition, a Bible Dictionary says, "The Middle Assyrian Laws, which date as far back as the early 11th century B.C., specifically addressed abortion. In these laws—a collection of legal codes including decrees of the Assyrian kings and Amorite legal customs (Tetlow, Women, Crime, and Punishment, 126)—abortion was considered a serious offense against the state..."[91]

Some people will argue from silence that the Bible does not expressly forbid abortion but an argument from silence proves nothing – as the Bible also says nothing about nuclear weapons, which does not mean that God must be for them. Speaking to this rhetorical fallacy, one theologian says, "The most significant thing about abortion legislation in Biblical law is that there is none. It was so unthinkable that an Israelite woman should desire an abortion that there was no need to mention this offense in the criminal code."[92] The question is then asked and answered, "Why was abortion an unthinkable act for the ancient Israelites?" First, children were recognized as a gift or heritage from the Lord.[a] Second, God was seen to be the One who opens the womb and allows conception.[b] Third, childlessness was thought to be a curse, for the husband's family name could not be carried on.[c] Barrenness meant the extinction of the family name.[d] Induced abortion was so abhorrent to the Israelite

---

[a] Gen. 33:5; Ps. 113:9; 127:3 [b] Gen. 29:33; 30:22; 1 Sam. 1:19–20 [c] Deut. 25:6; Ruth 4:5 [d] cf. Jer. 11:19

mind that it was not necessary to have a specific prohibition to deal with it in the Law. Sufficient was the command, "You shall not murder".[a],[93]

If you are reading these arguments for life and claim to be a Christian, but are still not convinced, I would ask you to consider what your reasoned defense of abortion might be. Considering the mounting mountain of evidence from science and Scripture, the burden of proof is on you to prove how the God of the Bible, the Lord Jesus Christ, could possibly support the taking of an innocent, unborn, vulnerable, defenseless human being. In our day of creedless critics and cancel culture, it's not enough to attack a person for their beliefs; you need to be a person who also places your beliefs in the public square of ideas to undergo the same scrutiny you apply to others. There is no reason in the mind from the Spirit that would allow a truly born-again person to continue in such deadly error and today is a good time to change your mind and heart by agreeing with the Bible. If you do not agree with God, you will agree with Margaret Sanger, who you will learn about next.

[a]*Exod. 20:13*

ROE V. WADE DEATHS

59,000,000

63,000,000

69,000,000

TOTAL POPULATION OF THE SMALLEST 27 US STATES

TOTAL POPULATION OF THE LARGEST 2 US STATES (CA + TX)

8

HOW THE WOMB BECAME A TOMB

Revelation 2:20-22 (ESV) —...I have this against you, that you tolerate that woman Jezebel, who calls herself a prophetess and is teaching and seducing my servants to practice sexual immorality...I gave her time to repent, but she refuses to repent of her sexual immorality. Behold, I will throw her onto a sickbed, and those who commit adultery with her I will throw into great tribulation, unless they repent of her works...

Growing up as a student in public schools, I was taught, like most kids, the theory of evolution. We were told that human life was not created by God in His image with love and grace but rather evolved thanks to time and chance from lower life forms.

Just like Christianity looks to Abraham as the father of our faith, we were told to look to Charles Darwin as the father of science. At the time, they curiously forgot to tell us the entire title of his famous/infamous book, *"On the Origin of Species by Means of Natural Selection, or the Preservation of Favored Races in the Struggle for Life"*.

Planned Parenthood founder Margaret Sanger quoted Darwin for her mission of reducing life through abortion saying, "In his Origin of the Species, Darwin says, 'There is no exception to the rule that every organic being naturally increases at so high a rate, if not destroyed, that the earth would soon be covered by the progeny of a single pair.' Elsewhere he observes that we do not permit helpless human beings to die off, but we create philanthropies and charities, build asylums and hospitals and keep the medical profession busy preserving those who could not otherwise survive. John Stuart Mill, supporting the views of Malthus, speaks to exactly the same effect in regard to the multiplying power of organic beings, among them humanity. In other words, let countries become overpopulated and war is inevitable. It follows as daylight follows the sunrise."[94]

Darwin not only believed that human beings evolved from animals, but that some people were more evolved than others saying, "At some future period, not very distant as measured by centuries, the civilised [sic] races of man will almost certainly exterminate, and replace, the savage races throughout the world."[95]

MALTHUS IS THE ABORTION MASTERMIND

This evolutionary bigotry is behind the nefarious history of racist abortions that began with Nazi mastermind Thomas Malthus (1766-1834). Shockingly, Malthus attended and later became a fellow at Jesus College, Cambridge, and was ordained as a minister of the Church of England. Yes, the father of the modern abortion movement was trained to be a Christian minister, not unlike Judas who was also with Jesus but never for Jesus and loved to take innocent life. His underlying false premise was that population growth will always outgrow food supply and that the best way to preserve and improve human life is to impose stern reproductive limits on those who are poor, sick, and disabled as well as ethnic groups who are less evolved than whites and therefore less fit. This racist agenda was first

Malthus

published anonymously in *"An Essay on the Principle Population as It Affects the Future Improvements of Society"*. His views became increasingly popular as he and others built upon his original misguided assumptions. Here are some of his most clarifying and concerning quotes:

"The power of population is so superior to the power of the earth to produce subsistence for man, that premature death must in some shape or other visit the human race."[96]

"Instead of recommending cleanliness to the poor, we should encourage contrary habits. In our towns we should make the streets narrower, crowd more people into the houses, and court the return of the plague."[97]

"It does not, however, seem impossible that by an attention to breed, a certain degree of improvement, similar to that among animals, might take place among men. Whether intellect could be communicated may be a matter of doubt: but size, strength, beauty, complexion, and perhaps even longevity are in a degree transmissible…As the human race could not be improved in this way, without condemning all the bad specimens to celibacy, it is not probable, that an attention to breed should ever become general."[98]

Malthusian ideology was the foundation for Nazi Germany. Scientific American Magazine says, "His scenario influenced policy makers to embrace social Darwinism and eugenics, resulting in draconian measures to restrict particular populations' family size, including forced sterilizations."[99]

It goes on to say, "In his book The Evolution of Everything (Harper, 2015), evolutionary biologist and journalist Matt Ridley sums up the policy succinctly: 'Better to be cruel to be kind.' The belief that 'those in power knew best what was good for the vulnerable and weak' led directly to legal actions based on questionable Malthusian science. For example, the English Poor Law implemented by Queen Elizabeth I in 1601 to provide food to the poor was severely curtailed by the Poor Law Amendment Act of 1834, based on Malthusian reasoning that helping the poor only encourages them to have more children and thereby exacerbate poverty. The British government had a similar Malthusian attitude during the Irish potato famine of the 1840s, Ridley notes, reasoning that famine, in the words of Assistant Secretary to the Treasury Charles Trevelyan, was an 'effective mechanism for reducing surplus population.' A few decades later Francis Galton advocated marriage between the fittest individuals ('What nature does blindly, slowly, and ruthlessly man may do providently, quickly and kindly'", followed by a number of prominent socialists such as Sidney and Beatrice Webb, George Bernard Shaw, Havelock Ellis and H. G. Wells, who openly championed eugenics as a tool of social engineering."[100]

As the world witnessed the horrors of Jews being slaughtered in large concentration camps, it is important to note they were considered less evolved and less fit for life. Those chosen for forced sterilization or death were considered either a mortal threat to the German race (the "subhuman" Jews), or racially inferior (Gypsies, those with physical or mental disabilities, Slavs, Pols, Jehovah's Witnesses, accused homosexuals, and those simply thought to be "asocial" such as the unemployed, homeless, and welfare recipients).[101]

SANGER IS THE ABORTION STRATEGIST

As the world fought against the demonic implementation of Malthusian ideas contrary to all Biblical teaching that all people equally bear God's image and are one race – the human race – descended from Adam and Eve, another significant person in human history and abortion made a calculated decision. Seeing that mass murder in concentration camps was unsuccessful to market globally, she chose to instead have mass murder in much smaller clinics spread out in the neighborhoods where the "less fit" could kill their children via abortion. Yes, Hitler brought death in concentration camps and Margaret Sanger brought death in clinics, both in an effort to reduce minority populations. Abortion clinics are little concentration camps. Trying to promote social Darwinism, Sanger set up the first clinics in the poorest and most ethnic neighborhoods to reduce the "less fit".[102]

Theologian Wayne House says, "In 1933 the magazine for Planned Parenthood, known in Sangers [sic] day as Birth Control

Sanger

Review, actually published 'Eugenic Sterilization: An Urgent Need,' by Ernst Rudin, Hitlers [sic] director of genetic sterilization and founder of the Nazi Society for Racial Hygiene."[103]

Furthermore, later that same year the magazine "published an article by E. A. Whitney, entitled 'Selective Sterilization,' which strongly praised and defended Nazi racial programs."[104]

Sanger saw birth control as the most effective way to eradicate "feebleminded" people, whose mental ability was less than that of a 12-year-old.[105]

In her own magazine, *Birth Control Review*, Sanger argued that the medical world, "should broaden its conception of its responsibilities to include the amelioration of eugenic, economic, and social problems through the application of medical knowledge."[106]

For Sanger, birth control and abortion were the best way to increase wealth, decrease undesirables, and usher in a better and brighter future for the more fit at the expense of the "less fit".

On October 16, 1916, Margaret Sanger founded the first birth control clinic in America, which would ultimately become Planned Parenthood. She has been honored in the Smithsonian National Portrait Gallery, and her exhibit extols her saying, "Sanger's crusade had much opposition. But by 1921, when Sanger founded the Birth Control League, her movement had begun to win adherents in respectable quarters. Adding to her life of controversy is her association with the eugenics movement-which included promotion of forced sterilization for those deemed mentally unfit..."[107]

In New York, Margaret Sanger Square honors her legacy, along with an award that Planned Parenthood has awarded supporters for nearly 50 years. Planned Parenthood says, "Our highest honor, the Planned Parenthood Federation of America Margaret Sanger Award, is presented annually to recognize leadership, excellence, and outstanding contributions to the reproductive health and rights movement." Winners include Nancy Pelosi, Hillary Clinton, Ted Turner, Jane Fonda, Phil Donahue, and Alan Guttmacher, among others.[108]

Sanger has been named by *Time Magazine* as one of, "The 20 Most Influential Americans of All Time". *Time* says, "By word and deed, she pioneered the most radical, humane and transforming political movement of the 20th and 21st centuries."[109]

The Director of the Center for Human Dignity at the Family Research Council provides a much different pro-life summary of Sanger's life. He says, "Recent articles have reported on an unearthed

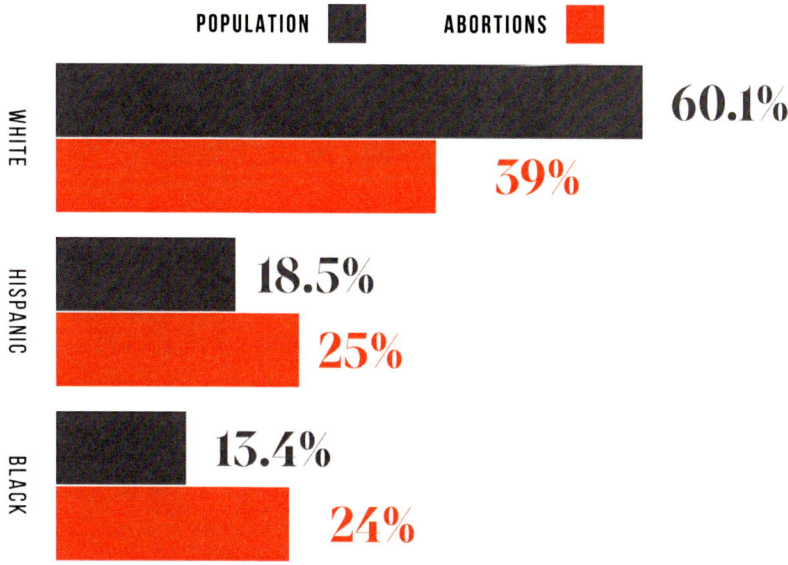

guttmacher.org, census.gov

video from 1947 of Margaret Sanger demanding 'no more babies' for 10 years in developing countries...Sanger shaped the eugenics movement in America and beyond in the 1930s and 1940s. Her views and those of her peers in the movement contributed to compulsory sterilization laws in 30 U.S. states that resulted in more than 60,000 sterilizations of vulnerable people, including people she considered 'feeble-minded,' 'idiots' and 'morons.'" She even presented at a Ku Klux Klan rally in 1926 in Silver Lake, N.J. She recounted this event in her autobiography: "I accepted an invitation to talk to the women's branch of the Ku Klux Klan...I saw through the door dim figures parading with banners and illuminated crosses...I was escorted to the platform, was introduced, and began to speak...In the end, through simple illustrations I believed I had accomplished my purpose. A dozen invitations to speak to similar groups were proffered".[110] That she generated enthusiasm among some of America's leading racists says something about the content and tone of her remarks.[111]

ABORTION IS WHAT HAPPENS WHEN THE DEMONS OF BIGOTRY AND DEATH CONSPIRE

We live in an age of cancel culture driven by the intolerista on the left who likes to dig up anything and everything anyone has ever said, take it out of context, and weaponize it in an effort to publicly crucify and bury someone so that their career, reputation, and influence can never resurrect. What is incredibly curious is that, if Margaret Sanger were connected to anything other than Planned Parenthood and the pro-abortion agenda of the fringe left, she would have been cancelled a long time ago.

Written in her sex education pamphlet "What Every Girl Should Know" that included chapters on body organs, sexual impulses and masturbation, sexual impulses in animals, and venereal diseases including gonorrhea and syphilis, Sanger says, "It is said that the aboriginal Australian, the lowest known species of the human family, just a step higher than the chimpanzee in brain development, has so little sexual control that police authority alone prevents him from obtaining sexual satisfaction on the streets..."[112]

One interesting and enlightening event in the life story of Margaret Sanger was her sit-down with veteran news anchor Mike Wallace for a free and frank interview. When asked by Mike Wallace, "Do you believe in sin?", Sanger said, "I think the greatest sin in the world is bringing children into the world--that have disease from their parents, that have no chance in the world to be a human being practically. Delinquents, prisoners, all sorts of things just marked when they're born. That to me is the greatest sin -- that people can... commit."[113]

Mike Wallace also asked, "What are your religious beliefs, Mrs. Sanger? Do you believe in God in the sense of a Divine Being -- who rewards or punishes people after death?" Sanger replied "Well, I have a different attitude about--the divine--I feel that we have divinity within us, and the more we express the good part of our lives, the more the divine within us expresses itself. I suppose I would call myself an Episcopalian by religion and there's a--many other, if you travel around the world you get quite a bit of the feeling of all... religions--have so much alike in the divine part of our own being."[114]

WOMAN AND THE NEW RACE

As a person who is, admittedly, a bit of a lightning rod for criticism and controversy, I have always appreciated people who at least attempted to understand what I actually believe, rather than taking bits and pieces of what I have said out of context, and creating a false narrative intended to malign and slander. If people disagree with me, I respect their attempt to at least seek to first understand me. As a general rule, I think most people feel the same about their critics.

In researching, I read a lot of original work from and interviews with Margaret Sanger who is the mother of what today would be the "gospel" of sexual feminism and abortion through the "local churches" of Planned Parenthood. I wanted to get to know her for myself, so I sat down to read her entire book *Woman and the New Race* to hear directly from her what she thought. I wanted to honor her by listening carefully to her underlying reasons for her radical revolution. Honestly, it was more frightful and evil than I would have even imagined. Here are some of the findings in summary with direct quotes from her that are consistent with their original context.

First, Margaret Sanger was completely convinced that the world was suffering from overpopulation. In her book, Margaret Sanger speaks repeatedly and favorably about Thomas Malthus and his eugenics ideology saying, "The Rev. Dr. Thomas Malthus, who died in 1798, issued the first of those works which exemplified what is called the Malthusian doctrine, also advocated celibacy or absolute continence until middle age. Mathus propounded the now widely recognized principle that population tends to increase faster than the food supply and that unlimited reproduction brings poverty and many other social evils upon a nation."[115]

In reading her entire book, it is plain that Sanger uses this flawed and now disproven "Malthusian doctrine" to advocate that eliminating the less fit, undesirable, and more savage was the most compassionate course of action for the benefit of humanity. She goes on to present this call to birth control and abortion much like a religious commitment saying of women who want to have large families, "Shall she not sacrifice her mother instincts for the common good…"?[116]

She also praises, "Robert Malthus, formulator of the doctrine which bears his name, pointed out, in the closing years of the eighteenth century, the relation of overpopulation to war…He demonstrated that were it not for the more common diseases, for plague, famine, floods, and wars, human beings would crowd each other to such an extent that the misery would be even greater than it is now."[117]

When Malthus was promulgating his fear-based lie in the early 1900's, the population of planet earth was roughly one billion. Today it is approaching 8 billion people. The myth of overpopulation has been disproven, and in many western societies the need is for higher birthrates to sustain nations who will go into decline if they do not see more children born, or more immigrants move into the nation. In recent years, the Pope and Elon Musk have repeatedly made this point, and it might be one of the few things they actually agree on because it is an established fact.

Second, Margaret Sanger was a strong advocate of moral relativism. Unlike Christianity, which teaches that there are fixed and unchanging moral laws from God, she believed and advocated that morality was to be established not top-down from God, but rather bottom-up from people in various cultures who could form and fashion their own sense of right and wrong in a fluid and changing fashion. In *WNR*, she establishes this worldview in the opening chapters of her book as a foundational conviction quoting Edward Westermarck and his most important work, *The Origin and Development of the Moral Ideas*, positively on this and other occasions. He is academically credited with the theory of ethical relativity which postulates that moral judgments are ultimately based on emotions in a person and not any external law from God or anyone else. This places right and wrong in the feelings of the individual and not in relation to any notion of God or divine law, which is the entire worldview of Christian ethics.

Third, Margaret Sanger ardently encouraged women to battle their longing to be mothers bringing life into the world in favor of limiting human population. She blamed women for the overpopulation that plagues the world saying in her chapter titled "Woman's Error and Her Debt", "Nor have family and plague been as much 'acts of God' as acts of too prolific mothers. They, also, as all students know, have their basic causes in overpopulation...While unknowingly laying the foundations of tyrannies and providing the human tinder for racial conflagrations, woman was also unknowingly creating slums, filling asylums with insane, and institutions with other defectives. She was replenishing the ranks of the prostitutes, furnishing grist for the criminal courts and inmates for prisons. Had she planned deliberately to achieve this tragical total of human waste and misery, she could hardly have done it more effectively... They went on breeding with staggering rapidity those numberless, undesired children who became the clogs and the destroyers of civilizations...War, famine, poverty, and oppression of the workers will continue while woman makes life cheap. They will cease only when she limits her reproductivity..."[118] Sanger even argued that infanticide was a stronger and deeper desire in a woman than motherhood saying, "If infanticide did not spring from a desire within the woman herself, from a desire stronger than motherhood, would it prevail where women enjoy an influence equal to that of men? And does not the fact that the women in question do enjoy such influence, point unmistakably to the motive behind the practice?"[119]

Sanger also supported the ancient philosopher "Aristotle, who believed that the state should fix the number of children each married pair should have" and goes on to praise him saying, "Aristotle was a conscious advocate of family limitation even if attained by violent means."[120]

Fourth, Margaret Sanger ardently opposed those people she considered less fit according to her evolutionary paradigm, "savage races", and others who are "defective".

Sanger said, "By all means, there should be no children when either mother or father suffers from such diseases as tuberculosis, gonorrhea, syphilis, cancer, epilepsy, insanity, drunkenness and mental disorders. In the case of the mother, heart disease, kidney trouble and pelvic deformities are also a serious bar to childbearing."[121]

Sanger also said, "No more children should be born when the parents, though healthy themselves, find that their children are physically or mentally defective. No matter how much they desire children, no man and woman have a right to bring into the world those who are to suffer from mental or physical affliction. It condemns the child to a life of misery, and places upon the community the burden of caring for it, probably for its defective descendants for many generations."[122]

Just because someone is different, does not mean they are lesser. Frida Kahlo became one of the most famous artists of all time despite being in severe pain and bedridden much of her life. John Nash struggled with schizophrenia as chronicled in the movie "A Beautiful Mind", but he won a Nobel Prize in Economics in 1994 thanks to his mathematical genius. Theoretical Physicist, Astrophysicist, Cosmologist, and Scientist Steven Hawking was diagnosed with ALS at the age of 21 and given just two years to live but worked until his death at age 55, despite being paralyzed from head to toe. Christian evangelist and motivational leader Nick Vujicic was born in 1982 with no limbs but today has a global ministry, Life Without Limbs, to encourage and help people with physical disabilities along with a wife and children. Andrea Bocelli was born partially blind, and at the age of 12 became totally blind, but went on to sell over 75 million records as a vocalist and musician. Michael J. Fox was only 29 when he was diagnosed with Parkinson's disease but continued to act and has raised over $230 million for Parkinson's disease research. Helen Keller was deaf and blind starting at 19 months of age and went on to be the first graduate with those limitations in the world, and her autobiography, *The Story of My Life*, is a classic in English literature. Franklin Roosevelt became paralyzed from polio and went on to serve as President of the United States, leading the nation through the Great Depression and World War II. Lewis Carroll had autism as well as deafness in one ear but penned beloved books including *Alice in Wonderland*. Musician Ray Charles was born into poverty during the depression to be abandoned by his father and raised by his sharecropping mother, started losing his sight at age five, and by age seven was blind, by age fifteen was an orphan, but went on to win seventeen Grammy Awards despite a decades long drug addiction.

How this kind of purported discrimination can be implemented boggles the mind. What qualifies as someone who is too physically or mentally abnormal to qualify for life? What about if someone is born, but then becomes "unfit" due to such things as injury or illness. Should we take their life for the greater good? In our culture that cheers the story of a person who overcame insurmountable odds to make something of their life, what right do we have to deny whole groups of people this opportunity, especially when so many other people are healthy and mentally fit but not making an effort to maximize the positive impact of their own lives?

Fifth, Margaret Sanger ardently opposed large families. In a chapter titled, "The Wickedness of Creating Large Families" in *WNR*, Sanger said, "The most serious evil of our times is that of encouraging the bringing into the world of large families. The most immoral practice of the day is breeding too many children" and goes on to press her case saying, "These statements may startle those have never made a thorough investigation of the problem. They are, nevertheless, well considered, and the truth…"[123] She then says, "The immorality of bringing into being a large family is a wrong-doing shared by three-the mother, the father, and society."[124]

Sanger attacked women with large families as a "brood animal"[125] and a "breeding machine and a drudge",[126] guilty of, "the most immoral practices of the day." Sanger also shockingly said, "The most merciful thing that the large family does to one of its infant members is to kill it."[127]

Sixth, Margaret Sanger was a racist by her own admission. In a chapter titled "Why Not Birth Control Clinics in America?" near the end of *WNR*, she says, "In conclusion, I am going to make a statement which may at first seem exaggerated, but which is, nevertheless, carefully considered. The effort toward racial progress that is being made to-day by the medical profession, by social workers, by the various charitable and philanthropic organizations and by state institutions for the physically and mentally unfit, is practically wasted. All these forces are in a very emphatic sense marking time. They will continue to mark time until the medical profession recognizes the fact that the ever increasing tide of the unfit is overwhelming all that these agencies are doing for society. They will continue to mark time until they get at the source of these destructive conditions and apply the fundamental remedy. That remedy is birth control."[128]

Sanger started "The Negro Project" in 1939 to expand birth control to southern black communities. She wrote the following to a program director, "The minister's work is also important and he should be trained, perhaps by the Federation as to our ideals and the goal that we hope to reach. We do not want word to go out that we want to exterminate the Negro population and the minister is the man who can straighten out that idea if it ever occurs to any of their more rebellious members."[129] [130]

The strategic Malthusian agenda implemented by Margaret Sanger continues as one report says, "79 percent of Planned Parenthood's surgical abortion facilities are located within walking distance of black or Hispanic communities. The Centers for Disease Control and Prevention's Abortion Surveillance report revealed that between 2007 and 2010, nearly 36 percent of all abortions in the United States were performed on black children, even though black Americans make up only 13 percent of our population. A further 21 percent of abortions were performed on Hispanics, and 7 percent more on other minority groups, for a total of 64 percent of U.S. abortions tragically performed on minority groups."[131]

Seventh, Margaret Sanger ardently opposed Christianity and Capitalism. Sanger also said, "Birth control appeals to the advanced radical because it is calculated to undermine the authority of the Christian churches. I look forward to seeing humanity free someday of the tyranny of Christianity no less than Capitalism."[132]

Throughout her writings, whenever Sanger does mention Christianity or the Christian Church it is always negatively. Sanger charged the Catholic Church with instigating, "the crime of bringing an unwanted child into the world". [133]

In a chapter titled "Woman and the New Morality" in *WNR*, she says, "Upon the shoulders of the woman conscious of her freedom rests the responsibility of creating a new sex morality...We get most of our notions of sex morality from the Christian church-more particularly from the oldest existing Christian church, known as the Roman Catholic. The church has generally defined the 'immoral woman' as one who mates out of wedlock...The church as sought to keep women ignorant upon the plea of keeping them 'pure'...It is within the marriage bonds, rather than outside them, that the greatest immorality of men has been perpetrated. Church and state, through their canons and laws, have encouraged this immorality. It is here that the woman who is to win her way to the new morality will meet the most difficult part of her task of moral house cleaning."[134]

She then goes on to quote Scriptures about marriage for the purpose of attacking them[a] saying, "If Christianity turned the clock of general progress back a thousand years, it turned back the clock two thousand years for woman" and then quotes an author who says, "Christianity had no favorable effect upon women."[135] She summarized her attack on Christianity saying, "Out of woman's inner nature, in rebellion against these conditions, is rising the new morality. Let it be realized that this creation of new sex ideals is a challenge to the church."[136] She also said in a chapter titled "Progress We Have Made", "The barriers of prurient puritanism are being demolished...A public whose thoughts and opinions had been governed by men and women engulfed in the old order has been shocked awake."[137]

Like a religious leader starting a new belief system that sounds a lot like the demonic Jezebel Spirit, she says, "The Woman Rebel, a monthly magazine, was established to proclaim the gospel of revolt."[138]

Lastly, she says, "womanhood is blasting its way through the debris of crumbling moral and religious systems toward freedom... what is the goal of woman's upward struggle?...toward the creation of

[a] *1 Corinthians 7:8-9; Ephesians 5:22-24*

a new race."[139]

A PASTORAL PERSPECTIVE ON MARGARET SANGER

As a Christian senior pastor preaching through books of the Bible since 1996, I have seen the cause-and-effect relationship between unhealed past trauma and present and future painful life choices. I'm not a trained clinician, but I've read numerous books on trauma, listened to lots of hours by professionals teaching about trauma, and witnessed it firsthand as a pastor trying to help people. If the debated reports of her involvement with theosophy, the Rosicrucian cult, and fortune tellers, along with atheism and abuse of alcohol and Demerol hold any truth, she was a profoundly troubled person.

I genuinely hope, despite her disdain for Christianity, that Margaret Sanger found forgiveness and newness of life and mind through Jesus Christ before she died. Admittedly hotly debated, it is believed that "Roe" who was the plaintiff in the historical abortion case herself converted to Christianity before she died, receiving forgiveness for her sins through faith in Jesus Christ. As the mother to three children, wife to two husbands, as well as numerous lovers, I do not know what drove Sanger's lifelong devotion to preventing and/or ending the lives of unborn children.

Time Magazine may have a clue in their praise of her ignoble life as noble saying, "Born into an Irish working-class family, Margaret Sanger witnessed her mother's slow death, worn out after 18 pregnancies and 11 live births."[140] She even dedicates her book *Woman and the New Race* which is her foundation and framework for her life's work to her mother saying, "Dedicated to the memory of my mother, a mother who gave birth to eleven living children."

In an interview with Mike Wallace, she admitted that her

mother was Catholic, which likely explained her refusal to use any form of birth control and her father was an atheist who had a lot of problems with the Catholic Church.[141] She went on to explain that her, "opposition is mainly from the hierarchy of the Roman Catholic Church."[142]

Working as a nurse, it makes one wonder if seeing women in "the poorest neighborhoods of New York City before World War I" under similar circumstances did not trigger some painful memories of the suffering of her own mother when she was a girl.[143] If so, then the pain experienced during her childhood might not excuse the pain she caused in her adulthood, but it would explain it.

As we near the end of this book, I must confess that it has been very difficult to write. For over a week following the first draft, I had trouble focusing, sleeping, and felt very oppressed. If you are a woman reading this and have had an abortion, person who has supported abortion, or are a man who drove his girlfriend, wife, or daughter to have an abortion I would expect reading this book has also been very difficult for you. As a pastor, I know many wonderful Christian woman who are pro-life, but have struggles and secrets of their own that a book like this can resurface and trigger them. If this has happened for you, it is an opportunity to pursue full forgiveness and healing by the God who not only gives life and birth, but gives new life and new birth. That is the heart behind the next and final chapter where we answer perhaps the most probing, painful, and personal question about abortion.

POSTSCRIPT: WHAT HAPPENS TO ME, AND MY BABY, IF I HAD AN ABORTION?

Revelation 21:4 (ESV) — "He [Jesus] will wipe away every tear from their eyes, and death shall be no more, neither shall there be mourning, nor crying, nor pain anymore, for the former things have passed away."

As a father and a pastor, I understand that this is a personal issue for many, if not most people. The first time I was confronted with the pains and questions that follow an abortion was from a young woman in the college ministry Grace and I ran as a newlywed couple having just graduated ourselves.

She was a bit of a shy young woman and after getting to know us a bit she asked me if I could answer a question for her. I was happy to do so, and was devastated by her personal and painful question, "What happens to me, and my baby, if I had an abortion?" As a teenager in high school, she apparently had a sexual relationship with her boyfriend who refused to wear a condom. Not wanting to disappoint him, and not clearly seeing his selfishness, she slept with him at least a few times before going to a clinic and getting on birth control without her parents' knowledge. The relationship did not last long…but she found out that she was pregnant with his baby!

Not wanting to have her Christian parents and church community know, she went back to the clinic without her parents' knowledge and had an abortion. Through heavy tears and deep weeping, she explained how painful, brutal, and awful the entire procedure was. She was told that it was simply a common medical procedure, so she was not prepared for the cramping and bleeding she had to privately manage while also dealing with guilt and shame.

By the time she was part of our college ministry, some years had passed, and she was walking with God as a faithful Christian. A godly young man declared his interest in her and wanted to begin dating her. She wanted to fall in love, get married, and one day have a family, but this possible romantic relationship triggered deep hurt from her past. She did not know if God could forgive her for what she'd done, wanted to know what happened to her unborn baby, and if she was disqualified from marriage, sex, and motherhood for her sin. She was not defending her decision but was devastated by her decision.

My wife Grace and I have had this conversation in various ways innumerable times over the years. The only reason one of my children was not aborted was because God saved them from me. I was sexually active as a committed, pro-abortion, non-Christian, as I said in the preface. I would assume that most people alive today could have the same thing happen to them as happened to this young woman.

Not only do people need answers, but they also need love, compassion, prayer, a listening ear, and an available friend. We cannot always fix things, but we can provide comfort and companionship. No amount of theology can compensate for the presence of somebody who does not try to answer all the questions or speed up the grieving process but is just there when you need them.

For those who have endured loss amidst loneliness, without a friend to provide comfort, I apologize for that double grief. And I would encourage you to use that dark season of the soul to compel you to use what you learned to be a comforter to others who are struggling as you were. You may not have had the friend you needed, but by God's grace you can become that friend to someone else, which can be a means of healing for you and the person you are walking with through their valley of the shadow of death.

In an effort to answer her questions in hopes of helping lift some burdens, here is the summary of what I said.

First, I told her that God loved her no more before her abortion and no less after her abortion. She was a true Christian, and God's heart for her was a loving Father's heart. He was grieved by her decision for her baby, but His love for her was based solely on grace and not on her moral works and performance, whether good or bad. God could not love her any more and did not love her any less. Those words seemed to comfort her.

Second, I told her that Jesus Christ forgives sinners, even those who take life. In fact, on the cross while dying, Jesus the Son of God prayed for those who were taking his innocent life saying, "Father forgive them." Jesus then died so that they, and we, could be forgiven saying, "it is finished!"

Third, I explained to her what happens to a baby who dies in the womb. This truth was comforting to her, and later also comforting to Grace and me when she miscarried our own baby. I told her that God decides who goes to Heaven, and that He can and does choose people from their mother's womb. Furthermore, Hebrews 4:15 tell us regarding Jesus, "For we do not have a high priest who is unable to sympathize with our weaknesses." Jesus knows life as a baby; Jesus knows what it is like to have someone you love die, as he wept at the death of his friend Lazarus; and He has suffered and tasted death. Jesus identifies with our frailty and humanity at every stage of human development: unborn, infant, child, adolescent, and adult.

Jesus—unlike any other concept of God—has empathy and insight for both the baby and those who love the baby and mourn his or her death. In Jesus, we have a God who relates to us and invites us to Himself for comfort and hope. More than just answers, He also offers His grace and presence.

Our God can also save us from the womb. Psalm 22:9-10 says, "Yet you brought me out of the womb; you made me trust you, even at my mother's breasts. On you I was cast from my birth; and from my mother's womb you have been my God." Examples of this in Scripture include Isaiah[a] and Jeremiah,[b] both of whom were called by God for prophetic ministry from their mothers' wombs. Also, in Luke 1:15, John the Baptizer was promised to "be filled with the Holy Spirit, even from his mother's womb".

Jesus welcomed children and said that His eternal kingdom was custom built for kids to be with Him forever. In Luke 18:15–17, we read, "Now they were bringing even infants to him that he might touch them. And when the disciples saw it, they rebuked them. But Jesus called them to him, saying, 'Let the children come to me, and do not hinder them, for to such belongs the kingdom of God. Truly, I say to you, whoever does not receive the kingdom of God like a child shall not enter it.'" This picture of Jesus welcoming children should be a great hope and comfort for parents who have lost a baby. The image of Jesus holding our miscarried child on His lap in His eternal Kingdom, waiting for our day of entrance into the Kingdom, is the single most comforting image that comes to mind when I ask myself what has happened to the child we lost.

The case study for the loss of a baby is in the Old Testament. 2 Samuel 12:15–23 tells the story of King David's child, who died very young, "And the LORD afflicted the child that Uriah's wife bore to David, and he became sick. David therefore sought God on behalf of the child. And David fasted and went in and lay all night on the ground. And the elders of his house stood beside him, to raise him from the ground, but he would not, nor did he eat food with them. On the seventh day the child died. And the servants of David were afraid to tell him that the child was dead, for they said, 'Behold, while the child was yet alive, we spoke to him, and he did not listen to us.

[a]Isa. 49:1–7 [b]Jer. 1:4–5

How then can we say to him the child is dead? He may do himself some harm.' But when David saw that his servants were whispering together, David understood that the child was dead. And David said to his servants, 'Is the child dead?' They said, 'He is dead.' Then David arose from the earth and washed and anointed himself and changed his clothes. And he went into the house of the LORD and worshiped. He then went to his own house. And when he asked, they set food before him, and he ate. Then his servants said to him, 'What is this thing that you have done? You fasted and wept for the child while he was alive; but when the child died, you arose and ate food.' He said, 'While the child was still alive, I fasted and wept, for I said, "Who knows whether the LORD will be gracious to me, that the child may live?" But now he is dead. Why should I fast? Can I bring him back again? I shall go to him, but he will not return to me.'"

David had hope for an eternal reunion in Heaven with his deceased child and so should we. Ultimately, the Father determines which children He will spiritually adopt into His family. This is His decision. It is not the decision of parents who have sent their children on to Him, nor the theologians who try and give a guarantee to grieving parents. The Father decides. And that is good news.

The same Father who sought me, saved me, and sealed me is the same Father I am trusting to do what is right and best with the baby we lost in miscarriage. And I trust Him. I trust Him fully. I trust Him completely.

In this matter, I find the doctrines of predestination and election to be greatly comforting. I am a father who worships a Father who seeks spiritual children who are unable to seek or find Him because of their spiritual deadness—but He finds them.

And while I do not have a clear promise from Scripture, I do trust my Father and am certain—by faith guided by Scripture and rooted in the character of the Father—that one day in His presence, by His grace, for His glory, I will hug my child. Jesus will wipe every tear from my eye, and I will weep no more because my Father has taken care of everything. I hope and believe the same thing for everyone who has lost a baby, no matter what their age or the cause of their death. I expect to see an incredible family homecoming in the Father's House and want you to not live under any shame, condemnation, or demonic torment but rather own whatever you have done wrong and give it to God for healing, grace, forgiveness, and I expect, eternal rejoicing. God is good, and even if we do bad, He remains good because that is who He is to us and our children!

Regarding this young woman, I am happy to report that she did marry a godly man, became a wonderful mother, and is today healed up and enjoying God's grace on her and her family.

If we learn anything from the story of the Bible, it's that God uses evil for good, and brings life out of death. The worst evil in history was the killing of Jesus Christ, and God used it for the greatest good and our eternal life. No matter what you have done, Jesus Christ has grace and eternal life for you. That eternal life does not begin the day you die, but rather the day you meet Jesus Christ as God and Savior. The Holy Spirit wants Heaven to come to you in this life, before you die and go to Heaven in the next life. Any guilt, condemnation, or shame that you have been carrying were already carried by Jesus Christ on your behalf to the cross. In His death is your forgiveness. In His resurrection is your new life. Jesus Christ is not just pro-life, He is pro-your-life!

ENDNOTES

1   https://www.washingtonpost.com/archive/opinions/1993/06/20/a-look-at-rove-v-wade-v-ginsburg-history-lesson-for-the-judge/6a8b1b10-0089-4b17-aec4-a17fc8d4bcf4/

2   Ibid.

3   Harvard Law Review, 87, 1, 7, (1973).

4   https://www.priceofroe.org/legal-scholarship/

5   Ibid.

6   https://www.cnn.com/2019/01/31/politics/ralph-northam-third-trimester-abortion/index.html

7   http://lib.tcu.edu/staff/bellinger/abortion/wolf-our-bodies.pdf

8   J. Carl Laney, "The Abortion Epidemic: America's Silent Holocaust," Bibliotheca Sacra 139, no. 556 (1982): 343–345.

9   J. Carl Laney, "The Abortion Epidemic: America's Silent Holocaust," Bibliotheca Sacra 139, no. 556 (1982): 343–345.

10   J. C. Willke, Abortion: How It Is (Cincinnati: Hayes Publishing Company, 1972), pp. 6–7.

11   J. Carl Laney, "The Abortion Epidemic: America's Silent Holocaust," Bibliotheca Sacra 139, no. 556 (1982): 343–345.

12   https://www.scientificamerican.com/article/how-medication-abortion-with-ru-486-mifepristone-works/

13   https://www.lawinfo.com/resources/insurance/pet-law/florida/if-my-dog-is-sick-and-will-not-get-better-can.html#:~:text=Abusing%20or%20neglecting%20an%20animal,criminal%20defense%20attorney%20right%20away.

14   https://www.lawinfo.com/resources/insurance/pet-law/florida/if-my-dog-is-sick-and-will-not-get-better-can.html#:~:text=Abusing%20

or%20neglecting%20an%20animal,criminal%20defense%20attorney%20right%20away

15 https://www.lawinfo.com/resources/insurance/pet-law/florida/if-my-dog-is-sick-and-will-not-get-better-can.html#:~:text=Abusing%20or%20neglecting%20an%20animal,criminal%20defense%20attorney%20right%20away

16 https://www.avma.org/resources-tools/avma-policies/avma-guidelines-euthanasia-animals

17 https://www.avma.org/resources-tools/avma-policies/avma-guidelines-euthanasia-animals

18 https://www.guttmacher.org/news-release/2018/about-half-us-abortion-patients-report-using-contraception-month-they-became

19 Walter A. Elwell and Philip Wesley Comfort, Tyndale Bible Dictionary, Tyndale Reference Library (Wheaton, IL: Tyndale House Publishers, 2001), 895.

20 Douglas Mangum, Miles Custis, and Wendy Widder, Genesis 12–50, Lexham Research Commentaries (Bellingham, WA: Lexham Press, 2013), Ge 22:1–24.

See Douglas Considine, ed., Van Nostrand's Scientific Encyclopedia, 5th ed.

21 See Douglas Considine, ed., Van Nostrand's Scientific Encyclopedia, 5th ed. (New York: Van Nostrand Reinhold, 1976), 943; Keith L. Moore and T. V. N. Persaud, Before We Are Born: Essentials of Embryology and Birth Defects, 6th ed. (Philadelphia: W. B. Saunders, 2001), 2; Bruce M. Carlson, Patten's Foundations of Embryology, 6th ed. (New York: McGraw-Hill, 1996), 3; Jan Langman, Medical Embryology, 3rd ed. (Baltimore: Williams & Wilkins, 1975), 3; Ronan O'Rahilly and Fabiola Müller, Human Embryology and Teratology, 2nd ed. (New York: Wiley-Liss, 1996), 8, 29.

22 https://downloads.frc.org/EF/EF21F56.pdf

23 Robert P. George and Christopher Tollefsen, Embryo: A Defense of Human Life (New York: Doubleday, 2008), 3–4. George is a professor of jurisprudence and director of the James Madison Program in American Ideals and Institutions at Princeton University and a former member of the

President's Council on Bioethics. Right-to-life arguments have typically been based explicitly on moral and religious grounds. In Embryo, the authors eschew religious arguments and make a purely scientific and philosophical case that the fetus, from the instant of conception, is a human being, with all the moral and political rights inherent in that status. The authors argue that there is no room for a "moral dualism" that regards being a "person" as merely a stage in a human life span. An embryo does not exist in a "prepersonal" stage that does not merit the inviolable rights otherwise ascribed to persons. Instead, the authors argue, the right not to be intentionally killed is inherent in the fact of being a human being, and that status begins at the moment of conception. Moreover, just as none should be excluded from moral and legal protections based on race, sex, religion, or ethnicity, none should be excluded on the basis of age, size, or stage of biological development.

24   L. B. Arey, cited by C. Everett Koop, The Right to Live; the Right to Die (Wheaton, IL: Tyndale House Publishers, 1976), pp. 29–30.

25   Ibid, p. 30.

26   https://www.princeton.edu/~prolife/articles/embryoquotes2.html

27   England, Marjorie A. Life Before Birth. 2nd ed. England: Mosby-Wolfe, 1996, p.31.

28   Moore, Keith L. Essentials of Human Embryology. Toronto: B.C. Decker Inc, 1988, p.2.

29   Cloning Human Beings. Report and Recommendations of the National Bioethics Advisory Commission. Rockville, MD: GPO, 1997, Appendix-2.

30   Dox, Ida G. et al. The Harper Collins Illustrated Medical Dictionary. New York: Harper Perennial, 1993, p. 146.

31   Walters, William and Singer, Peter (eds.). Test-Tube Babies. Melbourne: Oxford University Press, 1982, p. 160.

32   Langman, Jan. Medical Embryology. 3rd edition. Baltimore: Williams and Wilkins, 1975, p. 3.

33   Considine, Douglas (ed.). Van Nostrand's Scientific Encyclopedia.

34   5th edition. New York: Van Nostrand Reinhold Company, 1976, p. 943.

34   Dr. John Eppig, Senior Staff Scientist, Jackson Laboratory (Bar Harbor, Maine) and Member of the NIH Human Embryo Research Panel -- Panel Transcript, February 2, 1994, p. 31.

35   Sadler, T.W. Langman's Medical Embryology. 7th edition. Baltimore: Williams & Wilkins 1995, p. 3.

36   Jonathan Van Blerkom of University of Colorado, expert witness on human embryology before the NIH Human Embryo Research Panel -- Panel Transcript, February 2, 1994, p. 63.

37   Moore, Keith L. and Persaud, T.V.N. Before We Are Born: Essentials of Embryology and Birth Defects. 4th edition. Philadelphia: W.B. Saunders Company, 1993, p. 1.

38   Larsen, William J. Human Embryology. 2nd edition. New York: Churchill Livingstone, 1997, p. 17.

39   O'Rahilly, Ronan and Müller, Fabiola. Human Embryology & Teratology. 2nd edition. New York: Wiley-Liss, 1996, pp. 8, 29. This textbook lists "pre-embryo" among "discarded and replaced terms" in modern embryology, describing it as "ill-defined and inaccurate" (p. 12).

40   Carlson, Bruce M. Patten's Foundations of Embryology. 6th edition. New York: McGraw-Hill, 1996, p. 3.

41   Silver, Lee M. Remaking Eden: Cloning and Beyond in a Brave New World. New York: Avon Books, 1997, p. 39.

42   https://acpeds.org/position-statements/when-human-life-begins

43   Kischer CW. The corruption of the science of human embryology, ABAC Quarterly.

44   Eberl, JT. The beginning of personhood: A Thomistic biological analysis. Bioethics. 2000;14(2):134-157. Quote is from page 135. Fall 2002, American Bioethics Advisory Commission.

45   https://acpeds.org/position-statements/when-human-life-begins

46   https://www.ncsl.org/research/health/fetal-homicide-state-laws.aspx

47   ibid.

48	https://scholarship.law.stjohns.edu/cgi/viewcontent.cgi?article=1581&context=lawreview

49	https://www.hopkinsmedicine.org/gynecology_obstetrics/specialty_areas/fetal_therapy/fetal-interventions-procedures/

50	https://www.congress.gov/bill/117th-congress/senate-bill/4132/text

51	Ibid.

52	https://medical-dictionary.thefreedictionary.com/fetal+viability

53	https://www.factcheck.org/2019/03/the-facts-on-the-born-alive-debate/

54	https://www.govinfo.gov/content/pkg/CRPT-107hrpt186/html/CRPT-107hrpt186.htm

55	https://www.nytimes.com/2022/04/01/nyregion/eric-adams-mask-mandate-children.html

56	https://data.unicef.org/topic/child-survival/covid-19/

57	https://www.uab.edu/news/health/item/12427-uab-hospital-delivers-record-breaking-premature-baby

58	Nancy Pearcey, "Sexual Identity in a Secular Age."

59	Paul Ramsey, Basic Christian Ethics (Louisville, KY: Westminster, 1950), 250, emphasis in original.

60	For another helpful summary of these views see Millard J. Erickson, Christian Theology (Grand Rapids, MI: Baker, 1998), 517–36.

61	Alan Cairns, Dictionary of Theological Terms (Belfast; Greenville, SC: Ambassador Emerald International, 2002), 5.

62	Matthew S. Beal, "Ten Commandments," ed. John D. Barry et al., The Lexham Bible Dictionary (Bellingham, WA: Lexham Press, 2016).

63	David W T Brattston, "Abortion in the Bible," The Churchman 108, no. 1–4 (1994): 354.

64	J. I. Packer, Knowing God (Downers Grove, IL: InterVarsity, 1973), 45.

65	Ibid., 53.

66	For the full summary and all of the specific journals and sources cited visit https://downloads.frc.org/EF/EF21F56.pdf

67	Kenneth L. Woodward, "2000 Years of Jesus," Newsweek, March

28, 1999, http://www.newsweek.com/2000-years-jesus-163776.
68   Kenneth Scott Latourette, "The Christian Understanding of History," Grace Theological Journal 2, no. 1 (1981).
69   Epistle of Barnabas, 19:5.
70   Stephen D. Ricks, "Abortion in Antiquity," ed. David Noel Freedman, The Anchor Yale Bible Dictionary (New York: Doubleday, 1992), 33–34.
71   Bakke, When Children Became People, 132–33.
72   Ehrman, Apostolic Fathers, 419.
73   Kapparis, Abortion, 48.
74   Bakke, When Children Became People, 133.
75   Kapparis, Abortion, 33–52.
76   Riddle, Contraception and Abortion, 3
77   J. Ryan Davidson, "Abortion in Antiquity," ed. John D. Barry et al., The Lexham Bible Dictionary (Bellingham, WA: Lexham Press, 2016).
78   F. L. Cross and Elizabeth A. Livingstone, eds., The Oxford Dictionary of the Christian Church (Oxford; New York: Oxford University Press, 2005), 413.
79   Athenagoras, Legatio 35 quoted at https://store.ancientfaith.com/abortion-and-the-early-church-by-michael-j-gorman/.
80   https://store.ancientfaith.com/abortion-and-the-early-church-by-michael-j-gorman/
81   Ibid.
82   Augustine, Marriage and Concupiscence quotes from https://www.newadvent.org/fathers/15071.htm
83   Alan Cairns, Dictionary of Theological Terms (Belfast; Greenville, SC: Ambassador Emerald International, 2002), 5.
84   Riddle, Eve's Herbs, 35, 68.
85   Riddle, Contraception and Abortion, 67.
86   Kapparis, Abortion, 7.
87   Riddle, Contraception and Abortion, 66–83; Kapparis, Abortion, 28.

88 Riddle, Contraception and Abortion, 66–83; Kapparis, Abortion, 28, 12–27.
89 J. Ryan Davidson, "Abortion in Antiquity," ed. John D. Barry et al., The Lexham Bible Dictionary (Bellingham, WA: Lexham Press, 2016.
90 https://www.ncbi.nlm.nih.gov/pmc/articles/PMC6027113/#:~:text=The%20Oath%20by%20Hippocrates%2C%20Translated%20by%20Francis&text=I%20will%20give%20no%20deadly,life%20and%20practice%20my%20Art
91 J. Ryan Davidson, "Abortion in Antiquity," ed. John D. Barry et al., The Lexham Bible Dictionary (Bellingham, WA: Lexham Press, 2016)
92 Meredith G. Kline, "Lex Talionis and the Human Fetus," Journal of the Evangelical Theological Society 20 (September 1977): 193.
93 J. Carl Laney, "The Abortion Epidemic: America's Silent Holocaust," Bibliotheca Sacra 139, no. 556 (1982): 346.
94 Margaret Sanger, Woman and the New Race. (New York, NY: Truth Publishing 2 Co., 1920), p. 48.
95 Charles Darwin, The Descent of Man (1871), Volume I, Chapter VI: "On the Affinities and Genealogy of Man," 200–201.
96 Thomas Malthus (2015). "An Essay on the Principle of Population and Other Writings", p.90, Penguin UK.
97 Thomas Robert Malthus (1989). "An Essay on the Principle of Population", p.115, Cambridge University Press.
98 https://books.google.com/books/about/An_Essay_on_the_Principle_of_Population.html?id=RWyFzNlColgC
99 https://www.scientificamerican.com/article/why-malthus-is-still-wrong/
100 Ibid.
101 https://encyclopedia.ushmm.org/content/en/article/mosaic-of-victims-an-overview
102 To learn more about the history of Planned Parenthood, read George Grant, Grand Illusions: The Legacy of Planned Parenthood (Nashville, TN: Cumberland, 2000).

103 Ernst Rudin, "Eugenic Sterilization: An Urgent Need," The Birth Control Review (April 1933): 102.

104 Leon Whitney, "Selective Sterilization," The Birth Control Review (April 1933): 85.

105 H. Wayne House, "Should Christians Use Birth Control?" Christian Research Institute, http://www.equip.org/site/c.muI1LaMNJrE/b.2717865/k.B30F/DE194.htm.

106 March 1917 issue of Birth Control Review, page 14.

107 https://npg.si.edu/object/npg_NPG.72.70

108 https://www.plannedparenthood.org/about-us/newsroom/campaigns/ppfa-margaret-sanger-award-winners

109 https://newsfeed.time.com/2012/07/25/the-20-most-influential-americans-of-all-time/slide/margaret-sanger/

110 Margaret Sanger, "An Autobiography," Page 366.

111 https://www.frc.org/op-eds/margaret-sanger-racist-eugenicist-extraordinaire

112 https://www.gutenberg.org/files/52888/52888-h/52888-h.htm is the entire document, and the quote can also be found at https://www.foxnews.com/politics/planned-parenthood-founder-margaret-sanger-controversial-history-center-abortion-debate

113 https://hrc.contentdm.oclc.org/digital/collection/p15878coll9o/id/27/rec/47

114 Ibid.

115 Margaret Sanger, Woman and the New Race. (New York, NY: Truth Publishing 2 Co., 1920), p. 31.

116 Ibid, 28.

117 Ibid, 27.

118 Ibid, 1-2.

119 Ibid, 5.

120 Ibid, 5.

121 Ibid, 27.

122 Ibid.

123   Ibid, 17.
124   Ibid, 21.
125   Ibid, 1.
126   Ibid, 16.
127   Ibid, 19.
128   Ibid, 62.
129   https://sanger.hosting.nyu.edu/articles/bc_or_race_control/. Not surprisingly, there is a rigorous debate about what she meant by that statement, though it has been authenticated as real
130   https://www.reuters.com/article/factcheck-pp-exterminating/fact-check-planned-parenthood-founder-margaret-sangers-1939-quote-on-exterminating-black-population-taken-out-of-context-idUSL2N2X11YN
131   https://www.frc.org/op-eds/margaret-sanger-racist-eugenicist-extraordinaire
132   David Goldstein, Suicide Bent; Sangerizing America (St. Paul: Radio Replies Press, 1945), 103.
133   Margaret Sanger, Woman and the New Race. (New York, NY: Truth Publishing 2 Co., 1920), p. 168.
134   Ibid, 50-51.
135   Ibid, 52.
136   Ibid, 53.
137   Ibid, 63.
138   Ibid, 64.
139   Ibid, 68.
140   https://newsfeed.time.com/2012/07/25/the-20-most-influential-americans-of-all-time/slide/margaret-sanger/
141   https://hrc.contentdm.oclc.org/digital/collection/p15878coll90/id/27/rec/47
142   Ibid.
143   Ibid.